Dilemmas and Decisions

To Janet

With love r best wishes

Patrick

8.4.18

CRITICAL ISSUES IN THE FUTURE OF LEARNING AND TEACHING

VOLUME 14

Editors

Britt-Marie Apelgren, *University of Gothenburg, Sweden*
Pamela Burnard, *University of Cambridge, UK*
Nese Cabaroglu, *University of Cukurova, Turkey*
Pamela M. Denicolo, *University of Reading, UK*
Nicola Simmons, *Brock University, Canada*

Founding Editor

Michael Kompf† (*Brock University, Canada*)

Scope

This series represents a forum for important issues that do and will affect how learning and teaching are thought about and practised. All educational venues and situations are undergoing change because of information and communications technology, globalization and paradigmatic shifts in determining what knowledge is valued. Our scope includes matters in primary, secondary and tertiary education as well as community-based informal circumstances. Important and significant differences between information and knowledge represent a departure from traditional educational offerings heightening the need for further and deeper understanding of the implications such opportunities have for influencing what happens in schools, colleges and universities around the globe. An inclusive approach helps attend to important current and future issues related to learners, teachers and the variety of cultures and venues in which educational efforts occur. We invite forward-looking contributions that reflect an international comparative perspective illustrating similarities and differences in situations, problems, solutions and outcomes.

The titles published in this series are listed at *brill.com/cifl*

Dilemmas and Decisions

A Critical Addition to the Curriculum

Patrick F. Miller

BRILL

SENSE

LEIDEN | BOSTON

All chapters in this book have undergone peer review.

The Library of Congress Cataloging-in-Publication Data is available online at
http://catalog.loc.gov
Names: Miller, Patrick (Patrick F.), author.
Title: Dilemmas and decisions : a critical addition to the curriculum /
    Patrick F. Miller.
Description: Leiden, The Netherlands ; Boston : Brill/Sense, 2018. | Series:
    Critical issues in the future of learning and teaching ; Volume 14 |
    Includes bibliographical references and index.
Identifiers: LCCN 2018007404 (print) | LCCN 2018009568 (ebook) | ISBN
    9789004368118 (E-book) | ISBN 9789004368095 (pbk. : alk. paper) | ISBN
    9789004368101 (hardback : alk. paper)
Subjects: LCSH: Education--Moral and ethical aspects. | Education--Curricula.
    | Decision making--Moral and ethical aspects.
Classification: LCC LC268 (ebook) | LCC LC268 .M527 2018 (print) | DDC
    370.11/4--dc23
LC record available at https://lccn.loc.gov/2018007404

ISBN: 978-90-04-36809-5 (paperback)
ISBN: 978-90-04-36810-1 (hardback)
ISBN: 978-90-04-36811-8 (e-book)

This book is printed on acid-free paper and produced in a sustainable manner.

Printed by Printforce, the Netherlands

To my wife and family

CONTENTS

CONTENTS

PROLOGUE

WHY DID I WRITE THIS BOOK?

Few would disagree with the generalization that "what we want to do in schooling is to prepare pupils for adult life" (O'Hear, 1981, p. 4), yet after 23 years teaching in secondary schools and 19 years as Principal of a Sixth Form College, I cannot but conclude that we are not very good at it. Leaving aside the regular (and often unjustified) criticism from the CBI (Confederation of British Industry) and local employers that too many students emerge without reliable basic skills in numeracy, literacy and technology, I would want to argue that of equal importance is the fundamental lack of preparation for taking marginal decisions in difficult circumstances where the outcome is not clear and the solution problematic. I believe that students need to learn to live with dilemmas, and this is the primary reason for writing this book.

It will be argued that there is no shortage of courses on critical thinking, materials on problem solving and "dilemmas" to discuss in the classroom. Books abound on contemporary problems; problem solving virtually begins in the reception class. But problems are not at all the same as dilemmas. Problems have solutions and disappear as soon as these are found. Dilemmas on the other hand leave you with an aftertaste and a sense of regret about the rejected alternative. I believe, therefore, that "Problem Based Learning" by itself does not adequately address this issue.

Secondly, there seems to be an increasing tendency amongst opinion leaders, from management consultants to religious fundamentalists, Heads of State to CEO's to strut about the world, with all the sensitivity of a hippo in a house of cards, telling us that dilemmas are no more than problems awaiting the "right" solution (and they just happen to have it). Such people preach a utopian vision of moral clarity and solutions.

Apart from being infuriating, smug and irrelevant as guides in the real world, I believe such counsel (and the fact that you can pay through the nose for it makes it worse) is profoundly mistaken. It is also dangerous. It encourages simplistic dogmatic thinking, with judgmental attitudes towards those who disagree with you. It breeds fundamentalism and undermines democratic values.

On the contrary, the choice is not between a false liberalism, which teeters endlessly and indecisively, on the one hand, and a totalitarian certainty on the other. The alternative to tolerance and dither, is not unblinking dogmatism, it is a conclusion based on the knowledge that all human judgment is subject to error, that opponents can be confronted with conviction but without absolute condemnation. Voltaire's lines are relevant: "I disapprove of what you say, but I will defend to the death your right to say it" (Tallentyre, 1907, p. 199).

Thirdly, as I see it, the situation has been made worse by a conceptual misunderstanding about the nature and even the existence of dilemmas. This would appear to be based on the traditional philosophical argument that genuine dilemmas cannot exist in a rational world. It is suggested that, though we may *feel* that they exist, burden us, drown us even, in reality they are problems that require clarity of thought, difficulties that await a solution.

The same thinking would treat education as some sort of preparation for University Challenge, the Brain of Britain or the many factual panel shows. We expose students to problems that need solutions, and the faster the better, facts that require to be recalled under pressure of time and quick mental responses. It all adds up to a mismatch between the education that is provided and the world in which we have to survive, in effect a pedagogical failure.

This should not be overstated. There is always a place for fast recall of facts, for acquiring specific skills, facing goals and meeting targets in the school years. And there are many who struggle to ensure that learning is for understanding, and to unpack teaching in ways that

> Give students access to the pedagogic reasoning, uncertainties and dilemmas of practice that are inherent in understanding teaching as problematic. (Loughlan, 2006, p. 6)

Understanding the nature of dilemma is therefore crucial and establishing the common sense position that genuine dilemmas do in fact exist was important at the outset. Otherwise the whole edifice comes crashing down because its foundation is false; it is a house built on sand.

The main purpose of this book therefore is to establish a case for using what might be called "dilemma thinking" far more prominently than is the norm today as a pedagogic tool, at every level of education, rather than focusing predominantly on "problem solving". So, in part this is a book about understanding the nature of genuine dilemmas and how essential it is to prepare for them during our school years if our education is to be effective. It has been written out of a longstanding interest in the way value judgments are decided and the process by which a choice is made between difficult alternatives.

TARGET READERSHIP

The primary target is the teacher educator and all those involved in developing a pedagogy of teacher education. Also it is aimed at those on B.Ed. and Teacher Training Courses, trainees and Newly Qualified Teachers, as well as experienced teachers in secondary and post compulsory education. It is also relevant to students of philosophy, politics, ethics or religious studies; it should be of interest to leaders of adult discussion groups such as the University of the Third Age (U3A) and church leaders. The Dilemmas from Classical Literature (Appendix) would be useful at all levels of education, especially for Further Education students.

NAVIGATING ONE'S WAY

Those who wish to understand the nature of dilemma (how it differs from a problem, whether it is always accompanied by regret or guilt) and to see a suggested typology would best concentrate on Chapter 1. Those interested in the argument that genuine "dilemmas" do not really exist at all and are really "problems" with available solutions might turn to Chapter 2 to follow the traditional rationalist arguments for and against.

Chapter 3 will be mainly of interest to those seeking the opinions and attitudes of teachers themselves in Secondary Schools. It draws on a research project undertaken by a volunteer group of ten staff over two years, then a survey of sixty Heads of Department in ten post sixteen colleges and their reactions to the idea of including dilemma thinking in their examination courses. It also includes a study visit to the USA, which set out to discover what some of their "top schools" did to encourage critical thinking and problem solving amongst their "gifted and talented". Chapter 4 seeks a basic justification for including dilemmas in the curriculum and would be of interest to those looking for an educational or philosophical rationale.

Three perspectives are then examined, the political (the so-called "dirty hands" dispute) the sociological and the psychological, which would be of special interest to those studying those subjects. Then, those interested in the positive outcomes of dilemma and how to live with marginal decisions will see some suggested coping strategies in Chapter 8. Finally, in the Appendix there is a list of well-known examples, taken from classical literature, which would be useful as an exercise at any level of education.

Learning to live with a marginal decision is one of the most important yet difficult lessons in life and to recognise and face dilemmas is an essential part of any job or career, whether in the office or in parliament, in the operating theatre or board room, within the family or in a war zone.

Far from exhibiting weakness, this attitude shows strength; it is arguably more defective to be blind to the views of opponents, unable to see both sides of an argument or insensitive to alternative strategies, than to be swiftly decisive, unmoved by other points of view. Those who train in leadership, and teachers in our schools and colleges, can sometimes concentrate so hard on being decisive, and on fast problem solving, that they quash the very ability to make an astute decision, or reach a perceptive solution in the first place.

In summary, this book can be described as an attempt to address the need for an education that adequately prepares students for the dilemmas and decisions required in adult life. The words of Postman and Weingartner (1971) are as true today as when they were first written:

… Good learners are emphatically not fast answerers …

Perhaps most importantly, good learners do not need to have an absolute, final irrevocable resolution to every problem. The sentence, "I don't know", does not depress them. (p. 42)

ACKNOWLEDGMENTS

There are so many friends and colleagues who have helped me over the years that it would be impossible to list them all. I am grateful to them for helping me to develop my thinking on the various aspects of dilemma with conversations long lost to the memory, discussions and arguments. Like forgotten meals, I have been sustained by them. I am also greatly indebted to those colleagues who volunteered to join a discussion group on dilemma: Graham Bartlett, Ashley Bowden, Basil Hunt, Tim Leach, David Lloyd, Bill Mclelland, Tom Mayhew, David Shaw, Joan Stevens, John Whitlock and Steven Wright. I enjoyed exchanging ideas with Larry O'Carroll and Vivienne Louizos and am indebted to David Shapiro for suggesting material on medical ethics.

More recently, I should like to thank friends who have helped and supported me: Keith Pound, David Dance, Mike Benton, Geoff Fox and Chris Thomson.

There was also the generous response by distant Heads of Department in post sixteen institutions, who were prepared to complete yet another questionnaire, commit thoughts to paper and share interesting ideas on the way conflict and dilemmas are considered in specific disciplines.

Above all, I would like to express particular gratitude for the encouragement of my original Supervisor, Pamela Denicolo, who kept the flame of interest alive when it was guttering to near extinction and showed enthusiasm when mine was flagging. Without this, it is doubtful if this study would ever have been completed. Finally my gratitude goes to my family for forbearance, encouragement and patience with yet another distraction.

INTRODUCTION

On the face of it, dilemmas are a common predicament, the staple diet of adult responsibilities; they occur in all walks of life (and, as I was to discover, in all school subjects and courses, not just the humanities); in fact we all experience them. The decision by France to ban the burqa in public is a typical example, with a long list of pros and cons to be considered. When students leave school or university, if they are fortunate, they will find employment; it will not be long before they are faced with a hard decision, one without a clear answer. It may be that they are required to promote and sell goods that they know to be faulty or dangerous. Or it may be that they witness an example of blatant discrimination. It is illegal, yet to blow the whistle would mean losing their job.

Medical issues are especially fraught: Many families must face the painful question, is euthanasia ever right, or is it always a case of murder at worst and manslaughter at best? If someone is terminally ill, lives in permanent pain, is judged to have little or no quality of life and has left evidence, perhaps a living will, which shows they would prefer to be put out of their misery to being artificially kept alive probably at increasing expense and dismay of their nearest and dearest, should they rather be assisted to die in dignity? Then there are the questions surrounding stem cell research, organ transplants, animal experiments, whether to operate or not, and allocating scarce resources. All these present a rich vein of dilemmas.

Personal relationships are also a minefield of dilemmas. To commit oneself or not, to break or not to break, to choose A or B or neither. Light opera and romantic novels are crowded with examples of the kind: "How happy I'd be with either were t'other dear charmer away" (*The Beggar's Opera,* John Gay, 1728, Act II, Sc. 13, Air xxxv).

It has been my conviction that education could do far more than it does to prepare young people, not only to solve problems quickly and competently, which is a common teaching strategy, but to make and live with marginal decisions. Critical thinking or timed problem solving and group discussions are inadequate on their own.

A MISMATCH BETWEEN EDUCATION PROVIDED AND THE WORKPLACE?

The question is, do schools and colleges adequately prepare young people for the situation that will inevitably meet them as they step on to their chosen career ladders, or the various roles and responsibilities they find themselves in? Do we adequately educate students to face dilemmas? Or is there not a contrast between the aims of education and the circumstances of the workplace? Is it not the case that education fails our young people in this respect? And will that not always be the case unless we include examples of dilemmas in our subjects and courses? The opposite seems to be the case. We expose students to problems that need solutions as quickly as possible, the faster the better, or facts that require to be recalled against a ticking clock.

Admittedly, there are many who argue that learning is for understanding and should be reflective (e.g., John Loughran in *Developing a Pedagogy of the Teaching Curriculum*, Routledge, 2006). In this way a faint voice may regularly be heard, pressing teachers to be open minded, in Dewey's words (1933):

> To include an active desire to listen to more sides than one, to give heed to facts from whatever source they come, to give full attention to alternative possibilities, to recognize the possibility of error even in the beliefs that are dearest to us. (p. 30)

It is, however, usually a whisper, not the norm. Our educational institutions are modelled on what has been called an Answerland view of the universe, where the ideal performer is one who solves problems against the clock, remembers facts and sees the solution to puzzles faster than his or her competitors. It is argued here that we need to remind ourselves in every generation to avoid what has been called "*the pitfalls of Answerland*" (Russell & Bullock, 1999, p. 135).

But do schools and colleges have the time for all this? In the last fifty years, economic and political pressures have increased relentlessly. Those pressures include the inescapable need for cost effectiveness, time constraints and the intense competition for academic achievement. The world of education shares these with business, politics and society as a whole, pressures which militate against a reflective education, constraints on the time that can be afforded to digress from the syllabus, to "read round" one's subject, to indulge in related issues and on subjects like "general studies". One can only watch this disappearance over the decades with regret, as it is no longer cost effective for management to "afford" the luxury of straying from the examination syllabus. This raises the question whether we are actually preparing young people for a working environment where decisions have to be taken in difficult circumstances, for a world of dilemmas in fact.

To make matters worse, on looking into it, I was astonished to find that the very existence of dilemmas has been denied by rationalist philosophers for over two millennia. This standpoint, which has dominated academic thought over the centuries, takes a tough-minded approach. It is prepared to admit that we all wrestle with problems from time to time, or experience feelings of guilt, regret, or confusion. But, we are told, that is all they are, feelings and experiences. To argue that real dilemmas, equal choices, exist is to assume an irrational world. From Aristotle and Aquinas to Kant or Mill the rationalist has denied that genuine dilemmas exist. He would argue that conflicts among moral obligations are only apparent and that they disappear with careful analysis. They are simply examples of misplaced emotion, muddled thinking and, they would claim, if you only reasoned logically, weighed the consequences carefully (or even prayed harder) the right answer would always eventually emerge.

If one asks, how are marginal decisions made? How do you decide? The rationalist may reply that it is obvious: it is by weighing carefully the pros and cons and reading the scales. This approach cuts through all the talk and dither, takes a tough line and says in effect, know where you stand, what you believe in and take the decision. Then, it can be argued, just put it behind you and get on with your life. To halt between opinions, hopping from one foot to the other, hesitating interminably is no more than a common human weakness, to be feeble, irresolute, and indecisive. Everyone knows what it is like to, say, buy a car, take a job, but then hanker after the one that might have been. So why make an issue out of it? Why bother writing about it?

The reason is that common sense sees it differently; there are genuine cases where the alternatives are equally balanced, where the cost weighs heavily on both sides. Experience teaches us that moral dilemmas are a reality, not just apparent, and, if we are of a reflective cast of mind, they can cause considerable feelings of confusion, regret and guilt.

AN OUTLINE AND SUMMARY

The way forward, it seemed to me, and the strategy adopted in this book was to start with a working definition, asking what one means by a "dilemma" as opposed to a "problem", in order to gain a deeper understanding of both the experience and the concept. This is followed by taking a look at various educational contexts, as seen by teachers. Chapter 1, therefore, consists essentially of a discourse on the nature of dilemma. It is suggested that there are everyday situations, for which all students whatever their ability should be better prepared, when we have to choose between two *equally* balanced alternatives. Then, having chosen, we find that we are unable to close the file on the decision and to move on; perhaps we are haunted by regret, guilt or even anguish for the alternative we rejected. It is therefore about making marginal decisions and living with them.

There is the story from classical antiquity of the young man who was much perplexed about whether or not to get married and takes his problem to the philosopher Socrates to ask his advice. Instead of receiving some words of practical wisdom from the great man he was given the stark reply: "whatever you do, you will regret it" (Laertius, 1972, p. 163). We call these situations dilemmas and the aim of this book is to make them more explicit in our teaching and learning.

The argument here is that students should learn more about their nature and realize the need for decision and perhaps action before any solution is found or even available. We need to discover ways of living with the uncertainty and psychological impact of regret and sometimes guilt because of the paramount importance of reaching a decision. One important distinction to make is that a dilemma is not the same as a problem; a problem always has a solution and it disappears when the solution has been found. Dilemmas on the other hand leave you with an after taste, a remainder. They can be moral, depending on your point of view about what is a moral question but they are never trivial (we wouldn't describe the choice of a breakfast cereal as a "dilemma"). Dilemmas present us with an urgent and serious choice. Although this widespread, probably universal, predicament varies from situation to situation, each shares a number of characteristics, so the chapter ends with a suggested typology of dilemma.

Chapter 2 looks at the challenge from some rationalist philosophers that genuine dilemmas cannot be contemplated in a rational world; they only appear to exist because in reality they are just problems, however complex, and should be resolved by careful thought and analysis. This argument needs to be tackled at the outset because, if true, it would undermine the whole edifice of this book.

So, the traditional arguments for and against the existence of genuine dilemmas are considered. Strong disagreement is expressed with the theoretical standpoint that the moral and other contradictions which are experienced in practice and described by thinking people are merely cases of confusion that can best be resolved by clarity of thought.

The preferred standpoint in this study has been that form of pluralism, which was described by Gaut as a *"reflectively improved version of common sense morality"* (1993, p. 29), also by Hampshire (1983, p. 20), Williams (1973, p. 175ff) amongst others. Pluralism, it is argued, conforms best to the observation that there are conflicting moral duties, not only between different cultures, religious standpoints and ethical positions, but even within the same tradition. Relativism and Situation Ethics allows for the same principle to be applied differently in different situations. For example, to tell the truth does not have the same force when applied to the parent as it does to the child. Hampshire's view that *"the capacity to think scatters a range of differences and conflicts before us"* (1983, p. 151f) neatly supports Billig's argument that common sense in our Western culture contains contradictions which are an essential prerequisite of the ability to think or debate at all (1988). Similarly, Gaut refers to an inherited "raft of moral convictions, which has been passed on to us by our parents and fellows from our culture, altered and refined by the common understanding of previous ages" (1993, p. 33f).

Other philosophical arguments against the existence of genuine dilemmas are considered but rejected. The rules of deontic logic (the study of concepts such as obligation, permission and prohibition), as Gowans has argued, do not rule out conflicting all-things-considered duties. Whilst they would make it incoherent to have two opposing "must" prescriptions, the fundamental challenge of a dilemma is that the subject has not yet reached the point of saying "I must". Agents are still at the stage of trying to decide between (at least) two "oughts", which it is not incoherent to compare. Often, in fact, it is the consideration of "all things" that itself gives rise to the dilemma (1987, p. 26).

Regarding the argument from remainders, it must be admitted that feelings of regret do not of themselves prove that anything is regrettable (Foot, 1983, p. 382) nor that anyone is culpable. The existence of remainders does not on its own establish the existence of dilemma. However, if we allow that in some cases guilt is appropriate, we indicate our belief that a genuine dilemma has been experienced. It may well be the case that guilt is sometimes irrational, that it is occasionally implanted by a persuasive speaker, or that it may be the result of an over scrupulous conscience. This is not the point at issue. The person who experiences the regret, guilt or remorse is convinced that his or her feeling is appropriate and, however much the rationalist may like to dismiss the assertion as subjective or misplaced, this can only be done by applying an external, and therefore different, standard, to prove the case. It may be that this standard is also subjective or misplaced but, while we dispute the issue, the person's guilt needs to be faced (and perhaps counselled).

In Chapter 3 various examples are taken from Secondary Education to illustrate the way we can prepare students to face dilemmas and decisions. My research included working on a project for two years with a volunteer group of ten staff looking at dilemmas in specific subjects, a study visit to the USA to see what some of the so-called top schools provided for their most able students, and a survey of Heads of Department in post sixteen colleges in the UK.

In the volunteer group, it was agreed to begin by looking in a fairly general way at the kind of problems students came across in their A level courses which were open ended and admitted several valid solutions. Each member of the group presented a paper in turn from the perspective of her/his own subject specialism. They addressed the question whether dilemmas were considered as part of the course in different subject disciplines and, if so, to what extent are they distinct? What kinds of opportunity occur in post 16 courses to develop the ability to recognize and resolve dilemma? What do different disciplines understand by dilemma?

The study visit to the USA covered six stays: in New York, Princeton, Baltimore, Virginia, Houston and San Francisco. My main interest was in how well their students were prepared for dilemmas and difficult decisions and it focused mainly on the strategies adopted by some of their leading schools on teaching their Gifted and Talented students. This chapter shows how the greatest emphasis was placed on Enrichment and Acceleration; mostly in the belief that good learners were fast answerers and the highest value was placed on problem solving and critical thinking.

This was later followed up by an enquiry amongst 60 Heads of Departments in ten post sixteen institutions in the UK. A letter was sent in which a dilemma was defined as "a situation in which a choice has to be made between at least two pressing alternatives, where there is no obvious solution" and examples were given of both moral and non-moral issues.

There was a surprisingly high response rate and many were positive, even enthusiastic about the matter; one said the questionnaire had jogged him into the realisation of the importance of the subject and several wished to be kept informed of any findings or outcome. In all, 19 different subjects were represented by the respondents. All, with one exception, acknowledged the existence and importance of dilemmas in their subjects.

The question is then considered (in Chapter 4) whether an educational rationale for dilemma can be found and the issue is described from the point of view of the school or college counsellor. This may be of greater interest to the teacher than to the student, but since the intention of this chapter is to argue the importance and value of including the recognition of dilemma in our teaching and learning programmes, in counselling and in the general entitlement for all students, it is obviously crucial to be confident of the basic principles which underpin this.

The aim is also to show the feasibility of doing this, even within current constraints, and offers suggestions for the different ways in which this may be done by teacher, tutor or counsellor.

Three perspectives are then taken, in order to illuminate the concept from different disciplines and to provide a strong supportive argument for the existence of genuine dilemmas. Chapter 5 takes that of politics and public morality. This is sometimes known as the "dirty hands" dispute; it raises the question of living with two apparently conflicting moralities, public and private and whether the moral obligations that a person acknowledges in a post of public responsibility conflict with those that the same person accepts in her or his private life.

Contemporary political problems are considered, such as: can lying to save one's skin be justified politically? Is public morality distinct from private belief and can the same individual hold both at the same time (A case in point is the resignation in 2017 of the Leader of the Liberal Democratic party)? Is there a problem about seeking a representative for public standards, who also inevitably holds a personal morality? Sections are included on compromise and expediency and on the dilemma of nuclear deterrence. Does the potential for mass destruction in modern nuclear warfare challenge the very notion of there being any such thing as a "just war"?

In the world of public responsibility, we are bound to have hard choices to make. We can either shrug off our moral compromises and decide that in the jungle all is fair, because it is a cold, Machiavellian world separated from the human atmosphere of ethical obligations; or, we can try to purge our guilt in a variety of ways. Either way, we have to live with our "dirty hands".

It is one of the most interesting dilemmas in ethical philosophy and there are numerous ways in which schools and colleges can prepare students for it, by school councils, mock elections and opportunities for public speaking and debate.

The purpose behind the perspective in Chapter 6 is to see what light can be shed on the subject by anchoring dilemma in its social and ideological context. It is suggested that dilemmas are not only a natural part of society but a necessary precondition of the development of common sense, for liberal thought and much we take for granted in Western democracies. Focusing on the views of Billig (1988) and the Loughborough Discourse and Rhetoric Group, it is argued that common sense grows only in a certain soil and that ideological dilemma should be regarded as essential for developing the ability to argue, to make comparisons and for the very existence of a thinking society.

Students are asked to consider the interesting suggestion that even the existence of contrasting proverbs helps this process: "*nothing ventured, nothing gained*", we say, but also "*look before you leap*"; "*absence makes the heart grow fonder*" but also *"out of sight out of mind"*; *"many hands make light work"* but then *"too many cooks spoil the broth"*; *"charity begins at home"* yet *"love thy neighbour"*.

This chapter offers valuable material for any discussion of the "democratic values" that we say we believe in and fight for. It argues that such dilemmatic contrasts are necessary if we are to learn how to think at all and that fireside wisdom, even though frequently contradictory, assists in the very development of our thinking and arguing processes.

> The contrary themes of common sense represent the materials through which people can argue and think about their lives, for people need to possess contrary themes if they are to think and argue. (Billig, 1991, p. 8)

In Chapter 7, the third perspective on dilemma is that of psychology and is intended to help students to understand their decision-making and the post formal stage of thinking. Unlike the philosophical perspective, which is concerned mainly with meaning, consistency and rationale, or the sociological perspective, which looks at the social preconditions, psychology sheds light on dilemma by focusing more on the processes of thought, and of cognitive development; it is more interested in the personal perception of dilemma and the moral awareness that this presupposes, than in the social context or environmental circumstances. It is, therefore, from this perspective particularly that we can consider the question of recognition, how students come to accept dilemma, to acknowledge valid alternatives, rather than simply to be aware of them.

It is interesting to consider whether or not the recognition and resolution of dilemma represents a special type of thinking. A brief and selective consideration is therefore given of such "types" as: problem solving, lateral, creative and critical thinking. Other related studies are considered, such as those theories which deal with different kinds of conflict: decision making, avoidance strategies, post decisional reactions such as cognitive dissonance, and guilt about the outcome or about the rejected alternative.

As the students referred to in this research are in late adolescence, a period with its own distinctive character, one question considered is therefore: can post formal operational thought be seen as the final stage of cognitive development or is there another "stage", a further development in adult reasoning? The line taken here is that the recognition of dilemma (i.e. the acknowledgment of valid alternatives) has much in common with certain aspects of adult reasoning such as the tolerance of ambiguity, openness to relativism, the acceptance of genuinely conflicting obligations, the influence of the specific situation and context. These are arguably the characteristics of mature thinking and the later phases in cognitive and ethical development.

Chapter 8 considers how to live with tough choices or marginal decisions; how it may not be possible to do good at the same time as save one's own soul; innocent criminals must sometimes be prepared to pay the just price (as in Camus' *Just Assassins)*. A conclusion to the question of how to live with "dirty hands" is put forward using Gaut's phrase a *"reflectively improved version of common sense morality"*.

It has been my experience that teachers are increasingly unwilling to spend their professional life on a treadmill, delivering outcomes and examination results and being treated accordingly, namely as functionaries of the system. There is a questioning, idealistic streak in all who set out to be teachers, a spark to be lit, opinions to be contributed. I believe that teachers are glad, even relieved, to be given opportunities to consider curricular issues (and not simply to implement them) and to have the chance of experimenting with alternative strategies without having their careers on the line.

The book therefore ends with the positive outcomes that can be derived by students from considering (and experiencing) dilemmas. It is suggested that teachers should prepare students by (a) learning to recognize what dilemmas are, how they differ from problems and in what situations one might expect to experience them; (b) accepting that solutions to problems, in the sense of correct answers cannot always be found to issues faced in daily life, at work or at home and therefore the need to live with marginal decisions, and (c) realizing the positive value of dilemmatic experiences.

Teachers will be aware that the skills of perception, awareness and understanding that are developed by learning how to recognize and resolve dilemmas have a positive spin off in academic terms as well as in preparation for leadership, initiative and enterprise. To give students the opportunity to adopt different perspectives, to experiment with a variety of arguments and to come to terms with conclusions that are not cut and dried but are sometimes finely balanced has many positive benefits not only in school and college, but in adult life.

In the Appendix a number of well-known dilemmas are provided. They may be found useful not only as classroom material but also for conferences or group discussions. These dilemmatic situations are drawn mostly from classical literature and ways are suggested in which these could be used with students. Questions included are: Ethnic conflicts, how do you live in one culture but adhere to another? Can you avoid getting "dirty hands"? (from Sartre's *Les Main Sales*); Do you accept "tainted money"? (from Bernard Shaw's *Major Barbara*); Do you have a "sacred duty to yourself"? (from Ibsen's *A Doll's House*) and *Sophie's Choice* (from Styron's novel, and the film of that name).

WHAT IS A DILEMMA?

Defining the Concept for Schools and Colleges

Key Points

- A working definition
- Dilemmas versus problems
- Remainders, regret and guilt
- Moral and non-moral dilemmas
- Favourable and unfavourable alternatives
- A typology of dilemma

A WORKING DEFINITION

If we are claiming, as we do, that students should be made aware of dilemmas in all subjects across the curriculum, it is crucial to begin with a working definition of what we mean. In a general sense, dilemmas are most obvious in the decisions of prominent people, generals, politicians, surgeons, head teachers and such like. For instance, the decision to go to war in Afghanistan or Iraq was undoubtedly dilemmatic at the time. Is it ever right to intervene in the affairs of another country, to effect regime change or to take up arms in the cause of human rights? The allocation of resources to the NHS furnish politicians and surgeons with daily dilemmas. Should leaders in a pluralist society follow a public morality or should they follow their own personal code? One can think of military leaders in time of war, politicians in time of peace or US Presidents at any time.

In fact, however, it would be seriously wrong to limit dilemmas to the great and the good; we all make marginal choices at some time, and must live with those choices. They occur just as frequently in everyday life, or in the classroom, when teachers react to multifarious daily situations, when we make decisions about jobs, about bringing up children, keeping promises, forming friendships, telling the truth, divorce and much else besides. They are the stuff of popular journalism, TV soaps and novels. Susan Howatch in *Glittering Images* portrays Archbishop Lang defending himself against a modernist's attack on his attitude towards the divorce laws:

> "Caught between the Scylla of my moral inclinations and the Charybdis of my political duty", declared the Archbishop, unable to resist a grandiloquent flourish, "I had no choice but to adopt a position of neutrality". (Howatch, 1986, p. 6)

© KONINKLIJKE BRILL NV, LEIDEN, 2018 | DOI 9789004368118_001

Tough choices and the consequences of taking them are the stuff of world news, serious drama, gossip, comedy, TV soaps and family feuds. They are inescapable. However inured we may have become to human tragedies, tsunamis, famine, poverty, civil wars, terrorist bombs and the gamut of humanitarian crises, the fact is that life and death decisions surround us every day. A working definition of dilemma can be given:

A particular type of predicament, which is experienced by everyone at some time or another and which occurs when the pressing alternatives available to us, or serious obligations we face, seem so evenly balanced that it is hard, and sometimes impossible, to make a choice.

In ordinary conversation we may speak of being "between a rock and a hard place" or "between the devil and the deep blue sea". We call it a dilemma. As Davidson (1980) put it:

> Life is crowded with examples of the following sort: "I ought to do it because it will save a life, I ought not because it will be a lie; if I do it, I will break my word to Lavinia, if I don't I will break my word to Lolita"; and so on. (p. 34)

In *Sophie's Choice* by William Styron (1979) a mother in a Nazi Concentration camp is permitted by the guard to save one of her two children from death but not both. She alone must make the choice. In Shaw's *Major Barbara* (1907) the heroine was caught in the choice between giving up her work on behalf of the poor and accepting money that might have come from profits on drink and arms manufacture.

Dilemmas are hardly trivial matters. The word would be wrongly used if it referred to the occasional irksome trifles in life, such as which travel route to take? Which hors d'oeuvres to choose? Which tie to wear? It is usually kept for intractable quandaries requiring urgent solution.

Originally, it had a precise meaning and referred to two and only two alternatives, each with unpleasant consequences. The Shorter Oxford English Dictionary defines a dilemma as "*a choice between two (or loosely several) alternatives which are or appear equally unfavourable*". If there were three alternatives, strictly speaking it would be a "*trilemma*" and, if four, a "*quadrilemma*"; many alternatives could be referred to as a "*polylemma*". Now, however, "*dilemma*" is the word for all cases.

DILEMMAS VERSUS PROBLEMS

When is a dilemma not a dilemma? The answer is, when it is a problem. Problems can be solved; dilemmas can only be painfully decided. The distinguishing characteristic of all problems is that, once solved, they disappear. A problem does not remain once it is resolved, nor leave you with a sense of loss or regret. "Dilemmas", on the other hand, require choices that will leave "remainders", in the form of regret, guilt or simply a poignant memory of personal involvement. A "dilemma" is not simply a problem with a difference; it is a distinct category on its own, one in which "whatever you do you will regret it". A problem may range from a straightforward brain teaser to a complex personal quandary, but it will always carry the presumption that there is a correct solution to be found; once this is done, any remainder felt will not be regret, or guilt or sense of loss but, if anything, will be a sense of satisfaction that the task has been completed.

This raises the question; does not the remainder depend on the person's subjective feelings rather than on the objective nature of the dilemma itself? On psychology not fact? This certainly seems to be the case. Take, for example, the classic story of the testing of man's faith (Genesis 22.1–12). God commands Abraham to take his son out and to sacrifice him on the mountainside as a burnt offering. Abraham has three incompatible convictions. (1) Whatever God commands must be obeyed and cannot be wrong. (2) God has in fact ordered him to kill his son. (3) Child sacrifice is morally repugnant, humanly speaking. If Abraham was the kind of person who cared little for morality but a great deal for religion, he might understand the moral dilemma but follow the religious duty of obedience. He would have no regrets. Alternatively, Abraham might be both deeply moral and religious. In which case, he might see the moral dilemma, struggle with it, but eventually follow the religious path. He would then be ashamed that he had forsaken the moral standpoint.

A dilemma describes one of two situations: the first appears to have no solution. In this case, the dilemma is described as "irresolvable" usually because there is no rational way of comparing the alternatives or obligations. It's a question of apples and oranges. They cannot be weighed against each other. This may be because the situation involves *two or more different principles*, such as loyalty to one's friend on the one hand and honesty on the other. Pluralists, who argue that such a variety of principles is a normal part of the reality of practical living (Hampshire, 1983, p. 151f), or a matter of common sense (Billig, 1988), would therefore say that these are irresolvable because they are incommensurable. This means that it is not merely difficult in practice to find a solution to the conflict but impossible in principle. Gaut (1993) gives the example of a mother whose son has committed a crime and he asks her to shelter him from the police (p. 35). In some cases, depending on his crime, she will know what she ought to do. But in others her duty will be unclear:

> In these cases the agony she may feel is a product of her recognition that she is caught in the vice of two independent moral principles – to save her son and not to harbour criminals – each of which is deeply embedded in a role she identifies with: as a mother and as a citizen. (Ibid.)

Another example, originally given by Plato (1974), is the problem whether or not you should return some weapons, which you have borrowed, to their owner who will probably use them to kill someone (p. 66). In this case the principle of promise keeping conflicts with that of life saving. How can they be compared? The situation is not so different when a knife (or porn magazine) is confiscated at school or college. Should property be returned to the rightful owner when it is likely to be misused?

3

Another type of dilemma, which can also be described as "irresolvable", is the conflict that arises when there are incompatible obligations derived from the same principle. Marcus (1980) puts it like this:

> Under the single principle of promise-keeping, I might make two promises in all good faith and reason that they will not conflict, but then they do, as a result of circumstances that were unpredictable and beyond my control. All other considerations may balance out. The lives of identical twins are in jeopardy, and through force of circumstances, I am in a position to save only one. (p. 125)

Similarly, there could be a situation in which a team of surgeons has the duty of trying to save the lives of both Siamese twins when they must, for practical reasons, choose between them. A single principle dilemma occurs whenever there are evenly balanced situations presenting symmetrical alternatives, such as the choice between two good applicants for a single vacancy. Donegan (1984) argued that such questions are not so much moral conflicts as practical problems. For example, from the fact that I have a duty to save either *a* or *b* it does not follow that I have a duty to save *a* and a duty to save *b*. (p. 35)

REMAINDERS, REGRET AND GUILT

The second type of dilemma could be described as in a sense "resolvable", that is to say, it is possible to find a kind of solution but that is not the end of the matter. If a dilemma is resolvable, it is taken to mean that a rational preference between the available alternatives can be given. This may be articulated in a variety of reasoned arguments: "option A has these favourable outcomes, which make it superior to option B". Or "moral principle X has priority over principle Y". Or it may simply be expressed as an intuition: "I know this to be the right course of action", perhaps through introspection or some form of insight (leaving aside for the present the difficulties in holding this position).

There are obvious objections to defining any dilemmas as resolvable. Isn't this a contradiction in terms? Surely the moment a solution is seen, the dilemma disappears? In fact, it turns out that it never was a dilemma in the first place; it was "a problem". One answer to this objection is that there are different kinds of "solution" and not all of them remove the dilemma completely. Sometimes, for example, in cases of extreme perplexity, a decision may be taken in desperation, spontaneously and with no attempt at reasoned deliberation. In these cases, the dilemma remains even though some relief may be felt at making a decision. The fact that a decision has been taken does not by itself eradicate the dilemma; it is possible that, although a decision has been taken, no real solution has been found. In this case the dilemma has remained unresolved.

Other dilemmas may be eliminated by finding a practical solution (for example, by accommodating two engagements). Sometimes one of the alternatives can be eliminated; perhaps a solution can be found by conducting further enquiry, or by finding a compromise between two seemingly irreconcilable points of view (for example, in national territorial disputes). Hegel (1975) saw the role of tragedy as being to seek a reconciliation in questions of moral conflict.

Each of these so-called solutions in theory cancels the original, apparent dilemma. Nevertheless, although it is clear, all things considered, that there is a preferable course of action, and that therefore theoretically the matter can be resolved, there are other occasions when, despite careful thought being given to the decision, there is some remainder attaching to the overridden obligation which makes the person feel a sense of regret, guilt, remorse or even anguish. It can be argued that these sentiments are often appropriate to the case and that therefore they establish the reality even of an overridden obligation; so, although there was a reasonable solution, the situation was indeed a "real" dilemma and perhaps continues to remain so. In these cases, the dilemma may be said to be resolved objectively but not eliminated subjectively (Statman, 1990, p. 206).

Diogenes Laertius tells the story of a young man who was much perplexed about whether or not to get married. He takes his problem to the philosopher Socrates and asks his advice. Clearly, he hoped to receive some words of practical wisdom and guidance from the great man; instead, however, he received the somewhat stark reply: "*Whatever you do, you will regret it*" (1972, p. 163).

Breaking a relationship is even more likely to leave regrets, guilt or remorse. Whether to terminate a partnership or not may be resolved by decision but this by no means cancels out the dilemma, either at the point of decision or subsequently. Norah, in Ibsen's *A Doll's House* (1958), is faced with the problem whether or not to leave Helmer, her home and her children. She struggles with herself and eventually decides she owes it to herself to return to her former home. Helmer thinks she is mad, and chides her harshly. "*All your father's want of principle has come out in you. No religion, no morality, no sense of duty ...*" Nora says, "*I must stand quite alone, if I am to understand myself and everything about me ...*" Helmer calls her, "*You blind, foolish woman! ... It is shocking. This is how you would neglect your most sacred duties*". Nora asks what they are. "*Do I need to tell you that?*", says Helmer, "*Are they not your duties to your husband and your children?*" Nora replies, "*I have other duties just as sacred ... duties to myself*". Even though her mind is made up, the dilemma remains. "*It gives me great pain*", she says to Helmer, "*because you have always been so kind to me, but I cannot help it. I don't love you any more*" (Act 3).

In each of these examples there is a "remainder", which continues even when the decision has been taken. In these cases the problem has not really been eliminated, nor a real "solution" discovered.

MORAL AND NON-MORAL DILEMMAS

Sometimes dilemmas seem more practical than moral; for example, when deciding on a contract, you have to choose which tender to accept, the cheaper or the one with the higher specification; or you must decide which of two clashing diary engagements you will keep (Foot, 1983, p. 382). The difference between a moral and non-moral dilemma is not always clear-cut, however. What one person will see as a moral obligation another may see simply as a question of practicality. For instance, some people make a distinction between moral problems and contingent questions (such as which of two clashing appointments to keep); or professional issues (such as when a surgeon must decide on which operation is the best in the circumstances), or practical problems (to keep the old car or buy another). Although the case can be made that it is nevertheless crucial to make a distinction (Brennan, 1977, p. 55f), the fact that we usually ask, "which ought I to do?" does not automatically make it a "moral" issue. Nussbaum (1985) described the problem like this:

> The use of the two categories "moral" and "non-moral" suggests to numerous writers on the topic that the cases to be investigated fall into two neatly demarcated and opposed categories. They accordingly structure their discussions around this sharp division. By contrast, in everyday life we find, instead, a complex spectrum of cases, interrelated and overlapping in ways not captured by any dichotomous taxonomy. (1985, p. 239; 1986, p. 27f)

Leaving definitions aside, however, what all dilemmas have in common is that they constrain us to make an urgent and difficult decision. Moreover, each alternative carries with it an opportunity cost. It is therefore preferable, until shown otherwise, to accept each person's own description of his or her experience.

FAVOURABLE AND UNFAVOURABLE DILEMMAS

The next question which is frequently asked is whether a dilemma should be defined negatively or positively. The Oxford English Dictionary describes the alternatives as being equally unfavourable, but does it have to be so? Must it always have undesirable outcomes? Is it always the case that whatever you choose will have equally unpleasant implications? We have many expressions derived from common sense that would suggest this was the case: we speak of "jumping out of the frying pan into the fire", or being "in a cleft stick", "in a tight corner", or between "Scylla and Charybdis", or "between a rock and a hard place". There is a Latin saying which reinforces the same idea: "In front the precipice, behind the wolf" (quoted in Billig, 1988, p. 9). It is also interesting to see how many synonyms for dilemma carry a negative sense ("fix, jam, hole, mess" etc.).

It is possible, however, to reverse a negative dilemma simply by stating it differently and making it a choice between two positive outcomes. There is an example, in Aristotle's Rhetoric, of an Athenian mother who advised her son "Do not enter into public business; for if you say what is just, men will hate you; and if you say what is unjust, the Gods will hate you". To this Aristotle (1975) suggested the following retort: "I ought to enter into public affairs; for if I say what is just, the Gods will love me; and if I say what is unjust, men will love me" (p. 313).

Does this prove that dilemmas can equally well be expressed as positive alternatives? Aristotle may achieve a debating point with this argument, but it does not alter the fact that speaking justly or unjustly will in either case bear a negative cost. The decision to be taken may be between two equally favourable alternatives, but what makes us describe it as a dilemma is that each will have some undesirable cost; and if it is a moral dilemma that cost may be a sense of guilt.

Dilemmas may therefore sometimes appear to present favourable alternatives. Often they are expressed as choices between positive poles: deciding between two possible marriage partners, selecting which of two excellent candidates for a post, choosing between a job now with immediate income and further education with deferred advantages, these are all positive choices in themselves. However, in so far as dilemma is defined as a "situation" which has undesirable consequences as an opportunity cost benefit, it would appear correct to characterise it as unfavourable.

SUMMARY OF CHARACTERISTICS

To summarise, a list of characteristics, or typology, of genuine dilemmas can be drawn up. They describe situations, which:

- Are felt to be pressing and serious, and neither trifling nor inconsequential.
- Present evenly balanced choices or obligations.
- Make incompatible demands either within a single principle (such as not to lie) or between two different principles (such as saving life and breaking your word).
- Cause unfavourable consequences, that is to say whichever alternative is selected, an unpleasant post-decisional remainder is left behind, sometimes expressed as regret or guilt.
- Are distinguishable from problems in that only the latter leave no remainder and are properly eliminated when solved.
  May be seen by some as moral conflicts (e.g., is it right to kill in these circumstances?) and by others as non-moral, questions of practicality (e.g., which operation has fewest side effects?). Either way they require urgent decision.

DO DILEMMAS REALLY EXIST?

Facing the Sceptic's Challenge

Key Points

- The most intriguing problem of moral philosophy

Against

- Prioritism – differing obligations ranked in order
- Monism – conflicts within a single principle
- The argument from logical principles
- Guilt and regret are mistaken emotions
- Particularism – the moment of existential decision

For

- Examples from classical literature
- Pluralism and diversity
- Situation ethics
- The single value argument
- The argument from remainders
- The counter argument to traditional deontic logic

DO GENUINE DILEMMAS REALLY EXIST? – TRADITIONAL OPPOSITION

We would be failing students badly if we did not prepare them at school or college for the sceptical view that this is all a storm in a teacup and that, although problems clearly abound, awaiting solution, genuine unsolvable dilemmas are an illusion. The following chapter takes students through the main arguments against and the case for the existence of genuine dilemmas.

Despite the evidence from practical living or common sense, the astonishing fact is that most moral philosophers in the past have questioned whether genuine dilemmas, the conflict of ultimate principles, can actually exist at all. They argue that, whatever may appear to be the case, it is simply not possible that a person morally ought to do one thing and morally ought to do another, when both cannot be done. However, most people outside the academic world, would agree that what appears to be a "dilemma" refers to a reality so widely experienced that to be told it is irrational and wrongly named would be unacceptably artificial (and rather patronising).

© KONINKLIJKE BRILL NV, LEIDEN, 2018 | DOI 9789004368118_002

Depending on one's philosophical standpoint, different views are taken on this issue. For instance, if one's approach to ethics is rationalist (in the tradition of Plato, Aristotle, Aquinas, Kant or Mill) one's inclination will be to adopt a more restricted view of what constitutes a moral problem. The trouble about this is that once we start to narrow the definition of "moral", we can argue that there is always one alternative that is in practice preferable and so end up by denying the existence of moral dilemmas altogether. In a rational scheme of ethics to tolerate the existence of genuine moral dilemmas will seem to some like tolerating inconsistency (Donegan, 1984, p. 291ff).

On the other hand, others argue that moral concepts are "open textured" and that a rational scheme of ethics need not be so cut and dried, thus leaving room for dilemmas (Brennan, 1977). If you take seriously each individual experience, or you believe that ethical conclusions are reached mainly by intuition, you are likely to be convinced of the existence of genuine dilemmas. Even after clarifying misconceptions, errors and inconsistencies you are compelled to respect, in certain cases at least, the expression of regret, guilt or remorse. This remainder arguably provides good evidence that a genuine dilemma situation exists, because it has not gone away (Williams, 1973). It must be admitted, however, that others think that this is a faulty argument (Foot, 1983, p. 382; Conee, 1982, p. 9).

The Most Intriguing Problem of Moral Philosophy

Teachers may meet with a certain impatience with these arguments. But it is important to respect the two cases. The debate about dilemma, the conflict between moral duties, has its roots in classical thought but recently has been revived amongst philosophers. One wrote: "superficiality is perhaps more quickly revealed by what is said about this problem than in any other way" (Hare, 1981, p. 26). Another called it "the most intriguing problem of moral philosophy" (Raphael, 1974, p. 12).

It seems perverse that anyone should question this. After all, on the face of it, a conflict of duties is an every day experience so is it not a matter of common sense to recognize this? But opponents of genuine dilemmas do not deny that painful moral decisions have sometimes to be made or that serious perplexities are at the root of practical living. One accepts that there are such things as "knotty points" (Mill, 1910), another speaks of "competing considerations" (Conee, 1982) and all would agree that we are not able to avoid hard choices from time to time. Practical issues such as which of two promises to keep, which of two people to go out with, are certainly common enough, but the point is (they would argue) this does not make them genuine moral dilemmas; such perplexities are just evidence that life can sometimes be tough.

It will not do (so the argument goes) to say "there just are situations in which, whatever you do, you will be doing what you ought not, i.e., doing wrong". There are, it is true, some people who like there to be what they call "tragic situations"; the world would be less enjoyable without them, for the rest of us: we could have much less fun writing and reading novels and watching films, in which such situations are a much sought after ingredient ... In such a conflict between intuitions, it is time to call in reason (Hare, 1981, p. 31).

Misplaced Emotion, Semantic Confusion or Subjective Delusion

And this is the key issue: the use of reason; being rational about moral questions. Rationalism has been one of the most influential and pervasive traditions in our philosophical culture and it is Rationalist philosophers who have led the opposition to the idea that genuine moral dilemmas can exist. From their perspective, the idea of dilemma should be regarded as in some way incoherent and incompatible with moral reasoning. However, much they might sympathise with someone who was agonising between two alternatives, they would be more inclined to consider it a question of confusion, as if they were correcting a misspelling, seeing it as a kind of a logical inconsistency or an error in computation; a crooked argument, after all, can always be clarified by straight thinking.

On closer inspection, many so-called dilemmas can be discounted, and will turn out to be simply examples of misplaced emotion, semantic confusion or subjective delusion. Above all they are seen as irrational responses. One puts it:

> Moral dilemmas are of no special assistance in accounting for moral sentiments or in promoting good behaviour. And ... their existence would confound us with the prospect of impermissible obligations. The reasonable conclusion is that they are impossible. (Conee, 1982, p. 97)

Real dilemmas, therefore, simply do not exist and it would be better to stop using the term and regard such predicaments as painful but solvable problems. Instead, students should be taught how to live with difficult decisions and the resulting painful regrets (by toughing it out, perhaps). Those who claim to be "on the horns of a dilemma" must be missing something; the (rather irritating) assumption is that they are either too young, too uneducated, blind, confused, illogical, uninformed, emotionally involved or simply inexperienced to see the solution before their eyes. If, then, we "call in reason" and consider some of the arguments against the existence of genuine moral dilemmas, they can conveniently be grouped under five headings:

1. Prioritism – Differing Obligations Ranked in Order
The case here is that conflicting obligations can almost always be ranked in order of priority, and where they are of equal importance, they cancel out. For instance, Plato gives the example of the man who argued with himself whether or not to return a weapon to a potential killer. The choice, he thought, is clear: saving life has priority over keeping one's promise.

On the other hand, saving two children from fire, or keeping two promises, when in each case only one is possible, and there is nothing to choose between them –

these, so the argument goes, are not moral but practical problems, since there can be no moral requirement to carry out simultaneously two incompatible actions. Guilt, therefore, is an inappropriate reaction, however understandable.

Aristotle gave another method of ranking diverse and conflicting obligations in his Nichomachaean Ethics (1109a25–b15). According to him, the Golden Mean is the underlying principle of all the virtues and provides us with a means of prioritising them in any given situation. Every virtue, he considered, was a mean between two extremes, each of which was a vice. For example, generosity is the mean between profligacy and stinginess; pride, between vainglory and humility; courage, between recklessness and cowardice, and so on. (Truthfulness, seen as the mean between boastfulness and false modesty, does not fit so easily into this scheme.)

Aristotle considered all the virtues to be interdependent and rationally consistent with one another. The Golden Mean, therefore, becomes the priority principle for all the other virtues. It was, for example, impossible for someone to have one of the virtues but lack another because "the possession of the single virtue of prudence will carry with it the possession of them all" (op. cit. 1144a25). This implies a rational consistency amongst all virtues, which would preclude the possibility of ultimate conflict between them. At a practical level there may be room for argument but not at the level of "eternal facts". This is how he put the case:

> Surely nobody deliberates about eternal facts, such as the order of the universe or the incommensurability of the diagonal with the side of a square; nor about eternal regular processes … What we deliberate about is practical measures that lie in our power …

> We deliberate not about ends but about means. A doctor does not deliberate whether to cure his patient, nor a speaker whether to persuade his audience, nor a statesman whether to produce law and order, nor does anyone else deliberate about the end at which he is aiming. They first set some end before themselves, and then proceed to consider how and by what means it can be attained. If it appears that it can be attained by several means, they further consider by which it can be attained best and most easily. (op. cit. 1112b5–26)

From this it is clear that Aristotle allowed argument over practical issues, i.e. dilemmas of method, but thought that these could be rationally resolved by a consideration of what "can be attained best and most easily". In other words, prudence is the underlying principle and is therefore the ultimate deciding factor. He takes the case of the sea captain who was forced to jettison his cargo in bad weather in order to save his ship, the lives of his crew and himself. Although there is little doubt in his mind what he has to do, he nevertheless might regret the outcome for he is attached to the cargo. This, however, would be illogical. Prudence provides the solution to his apparent dilemma ("any reasonable person will do it") (op. cit. 1110a 4ff).

2. Monism – Conflicts within a Single Principle

The second argument that students will find being used against the reality of dilemma is the single principle or monist argument. Monism is the claim that there is only one source of moral authority (e.g., divine law) or one ultimate principle (e.g., utility) which supersedes all other principles. To illustrate this, examples may be found amongst the monotheistic faiths, such as Judaism, Islam or Christianity. In these religions, so it may be argued, the world was created by a God who ordered the laws of nature and whose essence includes both ultimate goodness and rational consistency. God created the laws for his creatures to perceive and obey. The fact that God commanded Abraham to sacrifice his son Isaac was a test of his obedience. It was not a dilemma; it was an absolute command and was in itself sufficient justification of what would otherwise be an abhorrent act. God is thus identified as the source of all moral law; conflict in the latter would imply confusion in the former. Therefore, in monotheistic religions, genuine dilemmas cannot exist.

According to St Thomas Aquinas, who nourished the rational attitude in theology, dilemmas were impossible. Moral conflict, the view that a person can be required to obey two conflicting laws, would imply that God's laws could be inconsistent, and that therefore God himself could tolerate incoherence. But, in ultimate reality the moral law can have no imperfection. God's law has always been understood in both the Jewish and Christian tradition as perfect, pure and changeless (Psalm 119.89, 142).

Kant: A Conflict of Duties Is Inconceivable

Kant, deeply influenced by his mother, who died when he was fourteen, was schooled in the German Evangelical tradition but emphasised the rational perspective. He held that the one true religion comprises nothing but laws and principles (1960, p. 156) and, since it is of the essence of a principle that it can never conflict with another moral principle, it is no surprise to find that Kant declared roundly "a conflict of duties and obligations is inconceivable" (1964, p. 24).

The major premise in Kant's argument is that every action falls into one of three categories: it is either morally necessary, morally impossible or morally indifferent (i.e. permissible). These categories exhaust all the possibilities. It would therefore be illogical to say that an action could be both necessary and impossible (op. cit. 2.8). Furthermore, moral rules are unconditional imperatives, that is to say universal binding duties. If, therefore, a rule declares an action A to be necessary, it cannot consistently be the case that another rule could declare action B, which conflicts with A, to be necessary.

So what about our clear experience of conflicting obligations? Kant accepted that in practice we might feel by intuition that we had a moral conflict. This was, however, what he called an imperfect duty (Kant, 1964, p. 48). Perfect duties cover every specific kind of action. There can be no latitude in deciding how to obey these duties. They cannot conflict. But imperfect duties are different; they do not cover specific instances but rather general ends (for example, the pursuit of happiness could conflict in individual cases with the pursuit of honesty). He called these ends the "grounds" of duty. When therefore it appears that we are faced with a dilemma of conflicting duties, one of them is not our genuine "perfect" duty. When a "ground" of duty is compared with a "perfect" duty" it retires from the field; it is weaker and ceases to be binding on us (op. cit. p. 24).

The Single Standard of Utilitarianism
Another single principle or monist argument, which teachers are likely to find popular amongst students, is Utilitarianism, as for example developed by Mill (1910). Although proceeding from very different premises, Mill arrived at a similar conclusion about dilemmas to that of Kant; that is to say, he was able to accept practical conflicts in daily life, but denied that they were genuine dilemmas.

Mill made two fundamental claim: the first is that there can only be one standard of value. "If there were several ultimate principles of conduct", he wrote, "the same conduct might be approved by one of those principles and condemned by another; and there would be needed some more general principle, as umpire between them". Mill's claim was that there had to be a single principle "with which all other rules of conduct were required to be consistent, and from which, by ultimate consequence, they could all be deduced" (1974, p. 951). The second argument defined that principle as the standard of utility.

There are many varieties of Utilitarianism but the general position is that goodness consists in maximising happiness and actions should be judged by their results. The root principle of Utilitarianism is that one must assess the consequences, direct and indirect, of one's actions. Despite variations in how one should interpret the meaning of utility (whether as happiness or as goodness) it is agreed that an action is right if and only if the consequences have greater utility than the consequences of possible alternative actions. For example, in the case whether or not to bomb Hiroshima and Nagasaki, a careful examination of the consequences will, it is claimed, reveal which course would have the greater utility and benefit to mankind. From this standpoint, conflicting moral obligations are resolvable by appeal to the single principle of utility:

> There exists no moral system under which there do not arise unequivocal cases of conflicting obligation. These are the real difficulties, the knotty points both in the theory of ethics, and in the conscientious guidance of personal conduct. (But) ... If utility is the ultimate source of moral obligations, utility may be invoked to decide between them when their demands are incompatible. (Mill, 1910, p. 231)

Two Levels of Thought: The Critical and the Merely Intuitive
Another approach which denies the existence of genuine moral conflict is taken by Hare. In order to explain why dilemmas appear so convincingly in daily life, he introduced a distinction between two levels of moral thinking. Hare called the two levels of thinking, the intuitive and the critical:

Those who say, roundly, that there can just be irresolvable conflicts of duties are always those who have confined their thinking about morality to the intuitive level. At this level the conflicts are indeed irresolvable; but at the critical level there is a requirement that we resolve the conflict, unless we are to confess that our thinking has been incomplete. We are not thinking critically if we just say "there is a conflict of duties; I ought to do A, and I ought to do B, and I can't do both". But at the intuitive level it is perfectly permissible to say this. (1981, p. 26)

Hare thus accounted for prima facie dilemmas but only at the expense of granting them any intellectual respect. Those capable of critical thought can resolve the apparent dilemmas, which so trouble the intellectually inferior!

3. The Argument from Logical Principles.
The third main line of argument against the existence of genuine dilemmas is derived from the logical principles of moral discourse (sometimes known as deontic logic). It is claimed that dilemmas are inconsistent with two fundamental premises. According to the first, if someone ought to do one thing and ought to do another, then that person ought to do both those things. Bernard Williams called this the principle of agglomeration (quoted in Gowans, 1987, p. 130). According to the second, if someone ought to do something, then that person can do that thing (Kant, 1964, p. 37).

But if, as is claimed by the upholders of genuine dilemmas, S ought to do A, and S ought to do B, then by the first principle S ought to do both A and B, and by the second principle, S can do A and B, which is clearly impossible otherwise S would not consider it a dilemma in the first place. Therefore, it is argued, moral dilemmas are logically inconsistent.

To put this another way, the logical application of deontic principles, it is said, requires that there can only be one *all-things-considered* prescription for action. To believe in the existence of genuine dilemmas is to believe that if a person really ought to do A (for example remain loyal to his country) and he really ought to do B (say, never tell a lie), then, he really ought to do both these things. And, since "*ought implies can*", what is being asserted is that he really can do both these things. This, however, is what has been denied. To believe in dilemmas, therefore, is to believe in a logical absurdity. A wayside pulpit puts it succinctly: "If you have conflicting duties, one of them isn't your duty" (quoted in Hare, 1981, p. 25).

This kind of logic has been applied to the case of the doctor who must choose which of two identical twins to save, given that he can only save one of them (Marcus, 1980).

Where the lives of identical twins are in jeopardy and I can save one but only one, every serious rationalist moral system lays down that, whatever I do, I must save one of them. By postulating that the situation is symmetrical, Marcus herself implies that there are no grounds, moral or non-moral, for saving either as opposed to the other. Why, then, does she not see that, as a practical question, "Which am I to save?" has no rational answer except "It does not matter", and as a moral question none except "There is no moral question"?

Certainly, there is no moral conflict: from the fact that I have a duty to save either a or b, it does not follow that I have a duty to save a and b. Can it be seriously held that a fireman, who has rescued as many as he possibly could of a group trapped in a burning building, should blame himself for the deaths of those left behind, whose lives could have been saved only if he had not rescued some of those he did? (Donegan, 1984, p. 308)

4. Guilt and Regret Are Mistaken Emotions.

The fourth type of argument attacks the idea that feelings of guilt, and other "remainders", are strong grounds for accepting the existence of genuine dilemmas (Williams, 1973). The Rationalist would argue that, no amount of feeling, guilt or regret, can possibly provide evidence for the reality of genuine dilemmas. Certainly, tough decisions may result in guilt or regret, but these do not establish the existence of genuine dilemmas. Post decisional feelings should not be used as proof. As Foot expressed it:

The form of this argument is surely strange … It is impossible to move from the existence of the feeling to the truth of the proposition conceptually connected with it, or even to the subject's acceptance of the proposition. (Foot, 1983, p. 382)

Conee similarly argued that it may be reasonable to feel regret in those cases where there are harmful results, but such regret does not substantiate moral dilemmas:

Feeling guilty is subjectively appropriate when the belief that one has failed which prompts the feeling fits one's moral principles. If your convictions include that every debt morally must be repaid, it is appropriate to your morality for you to feel guilty about defaulting. When someone does what is morally best while neglecting something his morality requires, his feeling guilty is therefore appropriate only because it is called for by morality as he sees it. It does not fit the facts. This sort of appropriate guilt does not imply that a moral mistake has been made. (Conee, 1982, p. 89)

This means that the only post decisional feelings which are ever appropriate are "relief (at escaping mistake), or self-congratulation (for having got the right answer), or possibly self-criticism (for having so nearly been misled)", but never guilt (Williams, 1973, p. 175f).

In the classroom or science laboratory, teachers will be familiar with the situation where students are allowed to make their own errors, watching them as they wander down blind alleys, set out on unproductive experiments, see problems where there are none (and vice versa). Indeed, there will often be sound pedagogical reasons for leaving them to follow their judgments, however mistaken, and to learn from the experience.

In a similar way, school and college counsellors will have observed clients worrying about problems that seem trivial from the standpoint of the interviewer; just as priests meet over scrupulous penitents in the confessional, reproaching themselves with feelings of sinfulness, counsellors hear expressions of guilt which they personally would regard as mistaken; if protestations of innocence do not by themselves deceive the wary tutor, why should apprehensions of guilt be any more persuasive?

From this standpoint, a teacher might decide that these subjective judgments should be corrected and clients counselled out of their imagined predicaments. After all, would it not be preferable for them to have their apparent dilemmas resolved in the light of wiser advice? Does not the individual conscience require tutoring? More important, could one not generalise from such instances and conclude that whenever a person experiences an apparent dilemma, it is in fact an example of confusion, an understandable emotion but a case of defective reasoning, blindness or mistaken definition?

5. Particularism – The Moment of Existential Decision

The final type of argument considered here, which may be called particularism, is taken from the famous example provided by Sartre (1948, p. 35). In L'existentialisme est un humanisme, a young man must choose between his patriotic commitment to the French Resistance and his duty to care for his aging mother. Sartre argued that ethical principles and systems are inadequate guides for action. We should therefore discard them altogether and improvise our own choices of action, without regret or remorse. It is in only in actually making the decision that an ethical obligation is created, and then only for that person and that situation. Prior to that moment, only a practical predicament exists, but no conflict of moral obligations and therefore no genuine dilemma.

To summarise, each of these five arguments against dilemmas contains a rejection of the actual (phenomenological) situation, implying in some sense that it is not a real state of affairs. A typical position is that of Conee, "There is no fact of moral life that cannot be accounted for at least as well without moral dilemmas, and their possibility would cast a shroud of impenetrable obscurity over the concept of moral obligation" (1982, p. 87). Counsellors and tutors would, therefore, need to be aware that in espousing these standpoints, they would be implying a failure of perception on behalf of their clients, who should be guided to use the power of human reason to see through their confusion and to develop the will to make the correct decision.

Those who followed these lines of argument would therefore find it hard not to direct students, to admonish the self confident, to interrupt the thoughtless, and to direct the aimless. If a dilemma is really perceived as the result of youthful inexperience or confused thinking, counsellors would have an obligation not to leave clients in their ignorance any longer than could be justified by the advantage to their educational or maturational development.

THE CASE FOR THE EXISTENCE OF GENUINE DILEMMAS

Nevertheless, teachers should help students to face up to and counter these arguments. There is no need for them to feel overawed or diminished by the rationalist case. There are many kinds of argument to support the case for the existence of "genuine" dilemmas, for example: "the argument from moral sentiment, the argument from a plurality of values, and the argument from single-value conflicts" (Gowans, 1987, p. 14).

A Comprehensive Shift in Perspective

Two preliminary points can be made. It is worth pointing out that the case in favour of the existence of "genuine" dilemmas entails a comprehensive shift in our perspective. It invites a new temper of mind, challenges us to think differently about the premises of our moral philosophy and invites us to ask fresh questions about accepted definitions. For example, the distinction between a moral and a non-moral conflict is less clear-cut, definitions are viewed as open textured rather than closed and complete, the different meanings of "ought" are distinguished and the universal claims of moral judgements are seen to depend more upon similarity of circumstances than upon identical rules.

Sartre and the Point of Decision

Secondly, in the previous section it was shown that Sartre tried to remove the ground on which genuine dilemmas stand. For him, ethical principles are created only at the point of decision, by each individual in each particular circumstance; therefore, there is no clash of principle for that individual and it can be said that there is no dilemma. However, by emphasising the point of decision, he actually supports the case for dilemma. There is no reason why the moment of existential decision might not be dilemmatic. Two moral intuitions might be experienced simultaneously, thus causing conflict to that individual. Therefore, Sartre (1948) makes it possible to reinstate the situation, seen in its entirety, as dilemmatic.

1. Examples from Classical Literature

In the first place, substantial support for the existence of genuine dilemmas can be found in classical literature and therefore opportunities to refer to it should be sought as often as possible. If it is questioned why one should choose examples which are "dead" and obsolete, one answer is that the very distance and the quality of the stories gives them the edge over more contemporary and apparently relevant cases. It is no surprise that dramatic literature, plays and novels deal frequently with individual dilemmas. The very messiness, the apparent incoherence, is the stuff of life and does not render it any the less "real" or objective; therefore dramatists have no difficulty in showing us dilemmas. In classical tragedy the existence of conflicting obligations is clearly seen, particularly in situations where, through fate or force of circumstance, good people cannot avoid evil actions because no guilt-free alternatives are open to them. Hegel (op. cit. p. 49) considered that the "general reason for the necessity of these conflicts" lay in the fact that:

> The substance of ethical life, as a concrete unity, is an ensemble of different relations and powers which only in a situation of inactivity, like that of the blessed gods, accomplish the work of the spirit in the enjoyment of an undisturbed life … The original essence of tragedy consists then in the fact that within such a conflict each of the opposed sides, if taken by itself, has justification; while each can establish the true and positive content of its own aim and character only by denying and infringing the equally justified power of the other. (Hegel, 1975)

For example, Sophocles' Antigone deals with conflicting duties, the familial and the civic; her choice lay between her family (and religious) duty to bury her brother Polyneices and her civic duty to obey Creon, the king. Creon had declared the burial illegal because Polyneices was a traitor to his city and honouring him would threaten law and order, while at the same time taunt those who had remained loyal. We can also note that Creon had his own dilemma and role conflict between his obligation as uncle and duty as king. Aeschylus in the Agamemnon considered the clash between paternal and military claims; Agamemnon is caught between his human feelings as a father for his daughter Iphigenia and his duties as a commander to his fellow countrymen to achieve military success. He is pulled in two directions by his divided sense of duty. Either way, Agamemnon cannot avoid doing wrong.

> What can I say?
> Disaster follows if I disobey;
> Surely yet worse disaster if I yield
> And slaughter my own child, my home's delight,
> In her young innocence, and stain my hand
> With blasphemous unnatural cruelty,
> Bathed in the blood I fathered! Either way,
> Ruin! (Aeschylus, Agamemnon, 160–184)

Other famous examples include: Brutus, in Shakespeare's *Julius Caesar*, who defends his murder of Caesar by saying that it was "not that I loved Caesar less, but that I loved Rome more" (Act 3, Scene 2); Nora, in Ibsen's *A Doll's House,* is torn between duties to her husband and "another duty, just as sacred … My duty to myself" (Act 3, Scene 2). Each of these dramatic situations is taking seriously the human experience. They do not necessarily expect a clear or tidy solution but reveal the phenomenology of dilemma at its most complex and heartfelt.

In Aeschylus and Sophocles, the sympathy of the audience is elicited by the Chorus on the grounds that, whatever they decide, the dramatic characters cannot escape some responsibility for the outcome; their hands are not entirely clean, remorse and reparations are expected from them.

Sometimes, as in the case of Oedipus, there are deeds too dark to be overlooked, even when performed by good people deciding for the best; even when forced by necessity, they are ensnared by a fate which decrees that, however scrupulously the path of virtue is followed, a terrible crime will be performed and a penalty is demanded. The Chorus will cry out for it in the name of justice. As the audience would have known well, the prevailing Greek moral code demanded that, when the gods required conflicting duties and evil resulted, human beings should both make suitable reparation and adopt an appropriate attitude. The fact that their snare was determined by the gods no more absolved them from guilt than belief in predestination exonerates a Calvinist. They are required to make amends, to adopt an appropriately humble stance. Clarity of thought, even when coupled with bravery in resolve, is not acceptable to the gods when accompanied by superficiality, glibness, or hubris. The Chorus, speaking as the conscience of us all, must remind Agamemnon of his proper attitude (Aeschylus, Agamemnon, pp. 160–184). Nussbaum (1985) concluded her discussion of Agamemnon's dilemma:

> Aeschylus then shows us not so much a "solution" to the "problem of practical conflict" as the richness and depth of the problem itself. (This achievement is closely connected with his poetic resources, which put the scene vividly before us, show us debate about it, and evoke in us responses important to its assessment.) He has, then, done the first thing that is needed to be done in order to challenge theoretical solutions to the problem.

> But if we recognize what he has put before us, we must recognize, too, that the solutions do not really solve the problem. They simply under describe or mis-describe it. They fail to observe things that are here to be seen: the force of the losing claim, the demand of good character for remorse and acknowledgment. We suspect that to advance toward a more decisive solution we would have to omit or revise these features of the description of the problem. (p. 266)

2. Pluralism and Diversity

Teachers can now move on to the cornerstone of the debate. The theoretical standpoint underpinning many of these examples from classical literature is that of pluralism, or the belief in the diversity of moral obligations. The moral prohibitions that people acquire, in various ways, are not instances of "one or … a very few injunctions, they are irreducibly plural" (Hampshire, 1983, p. 20). This view is held by such philosophers as Ross, Davidson, Nagel, Williams, Berlin, and Gaut. Pluralists have little difficulty in accepting the likelihood, even the probability of there being conflicting obligations. Variety in nature is to be expected, as Hampshire explained:

The capacity to think scatters a range of differences and conflicts before us: different languages, different ways of life, different specializations of aim within a way of life, different conventions and styles also within a shared way of life, different prohibitions.

A balanced life is a particular moral ideal to which there reasonably can be, and have been, alternatives acceptable to thoughtful men at different times and places ... My claim is that morality has its sources in conflict, in the divided soul and between contrary claims, and that there is no rational path that leads from these conflicts to harmony and to an assured solution, and to the normal and natural conclusion. (Hampshire, 1983, p. 20)

The theory that the capacity to think implies conflict and choice will be taken up later (Chapter 6) and in Billig's argument that the ability to debate and nurture common sense depends upon the existence of contradiction in society (Billig, 1988). It represents well the pluralist standpoint that there is a class of moral dilemmas in which there is a conflict of two fundamental principles. They are irresolvable because, being derived from a plurality of sources, they are incommensurable.

Another way of describing a fundamental conflict in reality is the Yin Yang theory of the universe, which Confucianists and Taoists have adopted. Originally formulated by Tsou Yen in the fourth century, the Yin and Yang are sometimes seen as night and day, darkness and light and symbolised in the circle divided into two pear shaped halves. In some explanations, the Yin is the female, passive and negative force, and the Yang is the male, active and positive force. They interact, permeating the whole universe as a conflict of opposites, a kind of eternal dilemmatic reality. Taoism is the belief that these conflicting opposites can be reconciled and transcended by Tao. This results, in practice, in the aim of letting things be; humility, non-interference are the best attitudes, and all efforts to intervene, whether by commercial competition, governments, war or political manifestos, are self defeating and impertinent.

The Parsis, whose religion, Zoroastrianism, teaches that two great spiritual forces, good and evil, exist in eternity, hold a rather different but equally fundamental view. God did not create, or permit evil, as in the Judaeo-Christian tradition. There is a permanent cosmic battle, in which humans must play their part and this conflict is a contemporary fact of life, as if one lived within a perpetual dilemmatic reality.

Another pluralist argument is that a collision of duties in particular cases was common. As Bradley (1927) wrote", every act can be taken to involve such collision" (p. 156). "The morality of one time is not that of another time" (p. 189). He thus disagreed with Kant that lying was always wrong. Sometimes there are "duties above truth speaking, and many offences against morality which are worse, though they may be less painful, than a lie" (p. 63). The ultimate good for every human being is "self-realization", which can take place in several ways, for example by fulfilling one's social role and the duties imposed by it. The conflict of duties that occurs as a result cannot be resolved by discursive reasoning or "reflective deduction" in order to arrive at a practical conclusion. Moral judgment is a matter of "intuition" or as he puts it: "To the question, How am I to know what is right?" the answer must be, By the αισθησις of the φρόνιμος [By the perception of the man of reason]; and the φρόνιμος is the man who has identified his will with the oral spirit of the community and judges accordingly" (p. 194).

It can be seen that pluralism has two characteristics: a belief in a diversity of first principles, which may conflict and make contrary demands in particular cases; and second, an absence of any explicit method to resolve them. There are "no priority rules, for weighing these principles against one another: we are simply to strike a balance by intuition, by what seems to us most nearly right" (Rawls, 1971, p. 34).

Diversity does not, of course, of itself entail conflict, although it makes it more likely. In theory, there could be a priority principle that enabled one to rank the different obligations, or even a permanent hierarchy of principles (such as duty to God, to one's country, family and self). Most pluralists, however, believe that no permanent priority principle exists at all. "Decisions about what to do must appeal to considerations about what is reasonable in the particular case, what is here best on balance, and require a sensitivity to aspects of the situation that resist codification" (Gaut, 1985, p. 18, cp Sartre, 1948, p. 35). Gaut called this process of reasoning "generative reflection" which she distinguished from "reflective equilibrium" – which, she argued:

> Merely adjusts intuitions to principles – since it involves an additional empirical claim about the conditions of generation, and can undermine some of our intuitions in a more radical way than is open to reflective equilibrium. (op. cit. p. 29)

Incommensurability

Pluralism has many implications for dilemma: one is the notion of incommensurability. If principles have different origins, it is difficult to compare one against another because there is no obvious standard to which to appeal (which is why Mill (1974) argued that logically we should need another "umpire" to decide between them; the pluralist would reply that, however convenient it might be to have an "umpire", life is just not like that). But being incommensurable does not mean we are reduced to inarticulate silence. It is still possible to provide reasons for one's decisions in a particular case. In theory we could not compare life saving with loyalty, honesty with promise keeping. In practice, however, there is normally little difficulty because other relevant factors assist us. Sinnott Armstrong calls these cases of "limited incomparability" (Sinnott-Armstrong, 1985, p. 321f). The fact that one cannot rank certain kinds of moral requirements (usually extreme instances) does not imply that one can never rank specific cases. A particular moral duty to one's family can be stronger than some moral duties to one's country.

Discussions on medical ethics have centred on "four principles plus scope" put forward by Beauchamp and Childress (1989). These are purported to be "a simple, accessible, and culturally neutral approach to thinking about ethical issues in health care" (Gillon, 1994, p. 184). The principles are beneficence (the obligation to provide benefits and to balance benefits against risks); non-maleficence (the obligation to avoid causing harm); respect for autonomy (the obligation to respect the decision-making capacities of autonomous people); and justice (the obligation of fairness in the distribution of benefits and risks). It is admitted that there is no set of ordered rules, no help if the principles should clash, but that we should "consider these in each case before coming to our own answer using our preferred moral theory or other approach to choose between these principles when they conflict".

In the correspondence generated by these arguments (BMJ 309, p. 1159f) several writers revealed some of the dilemmas that can emerge when these incommensurable principles conflict. For example, to practise beneficence and non-maleficence we need empirical evidence to assess the probabilities of harm and benefits. This is normally obtained by randomised controlled trials. Patients, however, who participate in randomised trials, would to some extent lose their autonomy unless they gave their consent. Yet, it is not often possible for them to be fully informed and it would seem that in those cases the principle of autonomy conflicted with the principle of beneficence.

The principle of scope offers another dilemma. The question arises whether those who do not participate should perhaps lose their right to treatment when refusing to assist the society that confers that right. Gillon replied to the first problem that full consent is not necessary, and, to the second, that such refusers should nevertheless always fall within the scope of deserving medical care. In this way, it can be seen that resolving a conflict between incommensurable principles requires us to refer the matter to another "umpire" (Mill, 1974, p. 951), perhaps the common sense of the agent. The fact of being incommensurable does not, as the debate shows, make resolution impossible, each person must use his or her own personally adopted standard to resolve the dilemma.

Irresolvable Dilemmas

Incommensurable dilemmas such those we have been considering, are often described as "irresolvable". But what might this mean? To resolve a dilemma may mean to eliminate the alternatives by proving that one of them has less force. After all, even choosing the lesser evil, assuming that one indisputably exists, is an absolute moral requirement; it is the "right" thing to do and solves the dilemma. Again, by resolution we could mean avoiding the choice altogether by procrastination; this is hardly a satisfactory solution, but inaction is not an uncommon response to a difficult decision. Then, again, resolution could also mean that the alternative obligations were reconciled in some way, which is what Hegel required of tragedy.

Two Meanings of "Ought"

There is another question which is implied by pluralism. Clashes between different "ought" statements are not necessarily conflicting recommendations for action. We have first to be clear what we mean by "ought". If it is an all-things-considered prescription to act in a particular way it would be inconsistent to believe that there could be two such final "oughts". An example would be the orthodox Roman

23

Catholic ban on contraception which applies equally to Christian, Moslem, Hindu or atheist. This is an absolute command, regardless of individual opinion or differences in circumstance.

Alternatively, "ought" may be a duty to do one thing if at all possible, an obligation with a built in *ceteris paribus* clause or, in other words, allowing for exceptions. Gowans (1987) described this distinction as between "ought" and "must" and considered it as a way of avoiding the inconsistency which, according to the principles of deontic logic, would otherwise exist:

> Thus, I will suppose that ought-prescriptions may conflict without inconsistency, but that must-prescriptions may not conflict; and I will suppose that the deontic principles govern only the latter. A must-prescription declares what is morally best and hence what, from the moral point of view, must be done. (p. 26)

Foot (1983) also makes a distinction between types of obligation, arguing that there are two senses of "ought". The first type expresses a moral "ought" that can conflict with other moral "oughts". Clearly this would result in a dilemma. The second type, however, expresses "the thing that is best morally speaking". Foot holds that it cannot be the case that a person both ought and ought not to do something in this second sense of 'ought' (p. 383f). One meaning expresses what is best morally speaking; clearly this cannot conflict with any other obligation without inconsistency. The other, however, expresses an action that ought to be done, other things being equal, or from the perspective of one among many moral values, a view congenial to pluralists. Such "oughts" can conflict, for they are not forbidden by the rules of deontic logic.

Epistemological Implications

Another related issue is the meaning of "reality" in respect of moral obligation. Does it represent a belief in an objective set of criteria, as most rationalists would claim, universalizable, provable by an observable state of affairs about the world? A pluralist would argue that the "reality" of moral values is the belief in a rationale for making a decision, a consistent procedure for reaching a conclusion, which applies to anyone else finding themselves in the same set of circumstances.

Brennan (1977), defending the cognitive stance, argued that it is not possible in the case of defining "right" and "wrong", to have an exhaustive list of criteria, as some rationalists tend to require, so that people know in advance what we mean. He gave as an example the word "unsafe"; no experienced mountain climber will have memorised a list of "unsafe" criteria because he must regularly be meeting unprecedented situations. It is the same, he argued, with moral terms. We do not travel with a handy check list of morally neutral facts to guide us. Nevertheless, just as a judge uses a wealth of "knowledge" to decide the relevance or otherwise of precedents, so also we are not forced to abandon a consistent, reasonable approach to deciding moral questions. Rather, it means that definitions are always open textured.

What the example from Brennan shows is that not all supporters of dilemma abandon the claim to cognitive, real or consistent descriptions of dilemma. What they do all have in common is the refusal to decide a priori against the possibility of holding consistent beliefs in dilemma.

Situation Ethics

Another implication of pluralism is that one must consider each circumstance separately and be prepared to adapt to it. This has sometimes been called "situation ethics" and is likely to find favour with a majority of students. A typical statement can be taken from Fletcher:

> There are various names for this approach: situationism, contextualism, ocasionalism, circumstantialism, even actualism. These labels indicate, of course, that the core of the ethic they describe is a healthy and primary awareness that "circumstances alter cases" – i.e. that in actual problems of conscience the situational variables are to be weighed as heavily as the normative or "general" constants ... The situational factors are so primary that we may even say "circumstances alter rules and principles" ...

> This is the temper of situation ethics. It is empirical, fact-minded, data conscious, inquiring. It is antimoralistic as well as antilegalistic, for it is sensitive to variety and complexity. It is neither simplistic nor perfectionist. It is "casuistry" (case-based) in a constructive and non-pejorative sense of the word ... It works with two guidelines from Paul: "The written code kills, but the Spirit gives life" (II Corinthians 3.6) and, "For the whole law is fulfilled in one word, "you shall love your neighbour as yourself" ... (Galatians 5.14)

> Christian situation ethics is not a system or program of living according to a code, but an effort to relate love to a world of relativities through a casuistry obedient to love. It is the strategy of love. This strategy denies that there are, as Sophocles thought, any unwritten immutable laws of heaven. (Fletcher, 1966, p. 29f)

A similar position was adopted by Bonhoeffer when he asked what is meant by "telling the truth" and what does it demand of us? He began by making a distinction:

> The truthfulness of a child towards his parents is essentially different from that of the parents towards their child ... consequently, in the matter of truthfulness, the parents' claim on the child is different from the child's claim on the parents ... From this it emerges already that "telling the truth" means something different according to the particular situation in which one stands. Account must be taken of one's relationships at each particular time. (Bonhoeffer, 1955, p. 326)

Pluralism Summarised

No better summary of the pluralist point of view and its implications has been given than by Gaut (1993). She called the belief in independent and diverse moral principles a "return to a common-sense morality" and used a powerful image to reinforce her point:

> From the pluralist's perspective, those philosophers who account for morality in prioritist terms, appealing to one underlying conception of the morally right, are like those urban planners who demolish the messily arranged structures of an old city that has evolved over centuries in order to place neat, ordered, planned tower-blocks in their place. The result in the moral case is likely to be the same as in the urban case: the area becomes uninhabitable. I have urged instead a steady programme of home-improvements, with the occasional demolition of a habitation when its foundations prove untrustworthy. I take it that this approach to ethics is only a return to common-sense: common sense morality. (p. 19)

Common sense morality is one form of pluralism. It has a set of principles, which fix one's prima facie duties (such as to keep promises, not to harm others, not to tell lies, etc.) These are universal in the sense that they apply in all cases which are identical in their non-moral properties. As Gaut explains: "To establish which principle is the more pressing in a particular context one uses … highly context-dependent reasoning and judgement … Having established which of the two conflicting duties is required in the circumstances, the duty is rendered absolute" What is required is a "reflectively improved version of common sense morality" (p. 33).

The Single Value Argument

A quite different case for the existence of genuine dilemmas, which is sometimes put forward, is the single value argument. Here it asserted by some (e.g., Marcus, 1980,) that a single principle obligation can give rise to an irresolvable conflict. For example, a doctor may not know which of two equally deserving patients he should treat (other things also being equal). A fireman may not be able to rescue more than one person from a blazing building. In Sophie's Choice the mother did not know which of her two children to offer to the camp guard. In each of these cases, it is alleged; the single principle (of life saving) gives no guidance as to which course of action to follow. No guidance means no solution and no solution means a dilemma exists.

The Argument from Remainders

A very different line of argument to support the case for dilemmas, which has already been referred to, was put forward by Williams (1973). In his view, leaving aside conflicts between a moral judgement and a non-moral desire, and the hypothetical possibility of holding two intrinsically inconsistent moral principles, Williams held that there are two basic forms of moral conflict. "One is that in which it seems that I ought to do each of two things, but I cannot do both. The other is that in which something which (it seems) I ought to do in respect of certain of its features also has other features in respect of which (it seems) I ought not to do it"; put concisely, the first is equivalent to: I ought to do a and I ought to do b, while the second is: I ought to do c and I ought not to do c.

Williams then went on to show that such moral conflicts are more like conflicts of desire than conflicts of ordinary factual belief. A rejected belief cannot substantially survive the point of decision that it was not true. But when we act on one of two desires, the rejected desire is not eliminated; "it may reappear, for instance, in the form of a regret for what was missed". This is a moral "remainder" and shows that even when we think that we have acted for the best, it would be a mistake to think that the rejected "ought must be totally rejected in the sense that one becomes convinced that it did not actually apply". Nussbaum (1985), sympathetic to this approach, pointed out that what is foregone

> may sometimes be peripheral and sometimes more central to our conception of good living, sometimes what is foregone adversely affects only the agent himself; sometimes there is loss or damage to other people ... sometimes the case may be self-contained, affecting little beyond itself; sometimes the choice ... may bring with it far-reaching consequences for the rest of the agent's life and/or other affected lives. Finally, some such cases may be reparable: the agent may have future chances to undo what has been done or to pursue the omitted course; sometimes it is clear that there will be no such chance. (p. 238)

This illustrates well the variety of situations which may occur leaving us with a persistent "remainder"; clearly some of the sentiments felt will be those of regret, guilt or remorse. Agamemnon may have had no choice, given his post, but the Chorus expected that, at the very least, he made some reparation and adopted a different attitude, just we might expect it from our politicians when driven to compromise. Others who support this type of argument include Marcus (1980), Fraassen (1973), Nussbaum (1985), and Statman (1990).

Justified and Unjustified Feelings of Guilt

It was shown earlier that rationalists considered that guilt feelings may be unjustified and, in any case, do not substantiate the existence of dilemma. Statman, realising that guilt feelings can sometimes be misplaced, being the result of an over scrupulous conscience, considered the attempt to make a distinction between unjustified guilt feelings and justified guilt feelings. This, however, involves us in a vicious circle. As he put it:

> It tries to establish the agent's guilt by the fact the agent feels justified guilt feelings. And how do we know that the feelings are justified? From the fact that he behaved wrongly and violated a (real) moral duty. But how do we know he

behaved wrongly etc.? From the fact he feels justified guilt feelings, and so we go round again. In other words, we could tell that guilt feelings are justified only if we already beg the question, and presuppose that the agent is guilty. (p. 198)

Nevertheless, his conclusion about the argument from sentiment is surely convincing, namely that even though one of the options which the agent faces is better (or less evil), all things considered, than the other (for example, a person might only be able to prevent a nuclear war and save millions of innocent lives by cheating, violating promises, betraying family and friends etc), "it would be very artificial to deny" that this is a case of a moral dilemma. Hence, some dilemmas are real, he claimed, even when they are resolvable. There may be a better thing to do (namely to prevent the terrible war) but it would be "ad hoc and begging the question" (p. 198) to deny that it was a moral dilemma. Nussbaum (1985) put the case well:

We have, then, a wide spectrum of cases in which there is something like a conflict of desires … We want ultimately to ask whether among these cases there are some in which not just contentment but also ethical goodness itself is affected; whether there is sometimes not just the loss of something desired but also actual blameworthy wrong-doing – and, therefore, occasion not only for regret but also for an emotion more like remorse. (p. 237)

Slote (1985) put the case that even the utilitarian can find a place for justified guilt. He asks us to imagine "an impersonally benevolent person who has devoted his (sic) life to helping people, but who learns that he has contracted a particularly virulent form of plague" (p. 164). Whatever he does, wherever he moves, he will infect people. There is no way of isolating him. Slote asked, "What will the conscientious person with utilitarian motivation feel about his actions if he learns that he has such a disease?" He concluded that such a person is likely to feel not only regret for infecting people, but also guilt about "what he has done (and cannot stop doing)". This, claimed Slote, illustrates a utilitarian moral dilemma.

Fraassen (1973) argued that guilt cannot easily be removed from the rejected obligation because it would make the doctrine of "Original Sin" incoherent. In the Old Testament, guilt is applied to several descendants of those Israelites who worshipped idols, "visiting the iniquity of the fathers upon the children, and upon the children's children unto the third and to the fourth generation" (Exodus 34.7). Similarly in modern times, many Germans are assumed to be guilty for the crimes of their predecessors. But is this convincing? "Original Sin" is a doctrine about the human condition, when faced with the perfection of God; it applies to everyone; it is not a doctrine about guilt for actual sins committed, still less is it an assertion about what people actually feel, a statement about human sentiments.

Guilt and Regret Distinguished
A more fruitful approach, and one that has been found to appeal to young people, it would seem, is to distinguish between guilt and regret. Even if none of the above

agents have any reason to feel guilt it would be natural for them to feel bad about not being able to do more, to save more; they might even feel guilty at the moment of explaining their choice to, say, a relative of the person who had died. What is justifiable, and surely unnatural to deny, is the feeling of regret. Agamemnon, Abraham or Sophie might be well advised to give up blaming themselves; they did what they had to do in the circumstances; guilt is not applicable. But it is reasonable for them to feel regret, even if they acted for the best in the circumstances. Thus it is not the case, as Marcus supposes, "you are damned if you do and damned if you don't"; that would indeed mean that the gods were irrational. But regret about being caught in such a web of circumstances, possibly some to which one contributed, is both natural and reasonable. Trigg stated the difference between guilt, or remorse, and regret as follows:

> To feel guilt or remorse one must think one has done something which is blameworthy at least in one's own eyes. It does seem odd to say that we feel guilty about being faced with a moral dilemma or that we feel remorse about having done something we regard as wrong when the only alternative was something viewed as a lot worse. It is not that we are being irrational. "Guilt" and "remorse" are inappropriate concepts to introduce here. If I do not blame myself I cannot be feeling remorse … Unlike remorse, regret can clearly be about events for which I am not responsible, even though I care about them. (Trigg, 1971, p. 48f)

A Counter Argument to Traditional Deontic Logic

There remains the problem of deontic logic. Are there rules that forbid the coincidence of two conflicting and genuine obligations? As pointed out above in the rationalist tradition it is held that the combination of the principle "ought implies can" together with the principle of agglomeration, (if you ought to do a and ought to do b, you have an obligation to do both a and b), renders genuine dilemma inconceivable. A number of recent philosophers have challenged this. Williams (1973) relinquished agglomeration and Lemmon (1965) argued against "ought implies can", but Gowans (1987) considered these moves to be mistaken; deontic principles stand or fall together, and as they rest on a single assumption his preference is to attack that premise.

The premise in question is that deontic modalities of obligation, prohibition, and permission and alethic modalities of necessity, impossibility, and possibility are analogous to one another. If ought expresses moral necessity, as Kant believed, then it indeed follows that moral dilemmas are impossible. Gowans, however, questioned why we should assume that the principles of deontic logic can be treated like the principles of propositional logic? Obligation and logical necessity are entirely different systems.

Nevertheless, to make the case that moral prescriptions never express necessity is difficult, because often it is clearly the case that an obligation is felt to apply come what may, whatever the circumstances. If, however, one considers that there are two kinds of moral prescription as did Foot and Gowans, then it opens the way to accepting genuine dilemmas. There are "oughts" which can never clash because they describe what one must do (in Gowans' preferred terminology "a must-prescription declares what is morally best and hence what, from the moral point of view, must be done"); there are also, however, "oughts" which may clash without being incoherent:

> An ought prescription declares, from the perspective of one among many moral values, that an action ought to be done. Hence, 'S ought to do A is always an abbreviation of 'from the perspective of such-and-such value, S ought to do A'. (op. cit. p. 26)

A similar conclusion is reached by Searle (1978): the belief that "I have an obligation to do A" cannot consistently be held with the belief that "I ought, other things being equal do B". On the other hand, there is no inconsistency between believing that one has an obligation to do A and the statement that, nevertheless, "I ought, all things considered to do B" (p. 87).

This has been a rather complex philosophical discussion necessary to underpin the personal experience of teachers, the practical examples and pedagogic debate that follows in the next chapters to which we now turn.

EVIDENCE FROM SECONDARY SCHOOL TEACHERS AND COUNSELLORS

Examples of Dilemmas across the Curriculum

Key Points

- Teachers and dilemmatic spaces
- Dilemmas across the curriculum
- Strategies in the USA for teaching the gifted and talented.
- Acceleration, problem solving and fast thinking
- Enrichment programmes
- Evidence from 60 Heads of Department in the UK
- The counsellor's viewpoint

TEACHERS AND "DILEMMATIC SPACES"

When looking for evidence of dilemmas in schools, it is appropriate to start with the personal experience of teachers themselves for they will frequently find themselves in what has been called "dilemmatic spaces" (e.g., Turner, 2016, 22, pp. 570–585). This is a concept, originally used by Honig (1996) in the field of politics, but developed by Fransson and Grannäs (2013), to describe situations in which there is often no right way of acting, but only a way of "acting for the best" (p. 5).

It may be that there is a clash between their personal standpoint on assessment and that required of them by examination policy; or it may be a conflicting interpretation between past history in that country and current political attitudes or perhaps there is a contrast between their own views on the goals of education and those of the school in which they work. Dilemmatic spaces are a useful concept, drawn from a wide range of disciplines such as social work, public service and political studies, to describe those predicaments:

> Dilemmatic spaces are social constructions resulting from structural conditions and relational aspects in everyday practices. The concept of dilemmatic space(s) makes it possible to approach what individuals construe as dilemmatic by adding space as a relational category to the concept of dilemma. Such an analytical move makes it possible to visualise how dilemmas emerge in a space between individuals and the context in which they find themselves.

© KONINKLIJKE BRILL NV, LEIDEN, 2018 | DOI 9789004368118_003

Within such a context, human relations, or more specifically, positioning and negotiation are seen as political actions. (Fransson & Grannäs, 2013, pp. 8–9)

The practical activity of teaching will often reflect the principles demanded by opposing theoretical positions. One such situation, the conflict between a transmission oriented education and a progressive, child centred one was described and analysed by Billig (1988). The problem, as he describes it, is "how to 'bring out' of children what is not there to begin with, how to ensure that they 'discover' what they are meant to" (p. 54). Using the dialogue in the Meno (Plato, 1956), Billig argues that the role of Socrates is similar to that of the classroom teacher:

He remains in control of the talk, governing the taking of turns at speaking, closing the boy's options even to an extent that we have not witnessed in schools, by merely inviting affirmations of ready-made propositions – the familiar 'leading questions' of the courtroom. The assumption implicit in Socrates' account of the process, that he will 'simply ask him questions without teaching him', is that questions do not carry information, that they may not inform and persuade, command and convince. Of course this is a demonstrably false assumption. (op. cit. p. 60)

Although Plato's theory of anamnesis can be distinguished from the use of "leading questions", Billig is concerned to make the point that the teachers he interviewed tried to find a place for both the progressive and the transmission orientated traditions and thus resolve their dilemma by practical compromise in any given situation.

Winter (1982) was concerned by a problem, which frequently arose in action research, namely the difficulty of summarising and analysing a mass of interview data from teaching practice. Finding widely used methods inadequate (analysis by content, themes or social science theory) "faithful to the views of students, classroom teachers, and pupils, as well as those of fellow supervisors", to their different aims, priorities and philosophical positions (p. 167). He wished to "evoke the main areas of tension in the situation without generating immediate controversy by seeming partisan", which would lead to the point of view being rejected. The formal theory underpinning this method, which he called "loosely" the sociological concept of contradiction, was:

That social organizations at all levels (from the classroom to the State) are constellations of (actual or potential) conflicts of interest; that personality structures are split and convoluted; that the individual's conceptualisation is systematically ambivalent or dislocated; that motives are mixed, purposes are contradictory and relationships are ambiguous; and that the formulations of practical action is unendingly beset by dilemmas. (p. 168)

He analysed each group of statements into a number of expressions of dilemma, tension, or contradiction, which he categorised as Ambiguities (tensions and awareness of complexities which do not require action), Judgments (courses of action which are complex, but not seen in negative terms – they are merely interesting) and Problems ("courses of action where the tensions and ambiguities seem to undermine the validity of the action, the rationality of the action required"). By means of this framework, he condensed the material into four "perspective documents", each one summarizing the responses of teachers, students, supervisors and pupils respectively. He concluded:

> My argument has been that this method produces an analysis, which is fully responsive to the concerns and definitions of interviewees. It retains something of the structural complexity of the original statements, and produces a thematic ordering whose coherence does not depend on academics' theories of practitioners' behaviour, not simply on researchers' hunches and prior commitments. (p. 173)

The irony is that teachers may not have the time or opportunity to prepare their students to cope with similar situations. They will therefore often personify the mismatch between what they have to teach and what they themselves experience, which is one of the main reasons for writing this book.

CONSTRAINTS AND PRESSURES

Before introducing any innovation, teachers will naturally ask what resources are available to them, how it has been received elsewhere and the attitude of staff in other institutions. This chapter looks at how a group of ten volunteer teachers discussed the issue of dilemmas in their particular subjects, in both science and the arts. Then a survey of the opinions of some 60 Heads of Department in the UK.

The main intention, as we have said, is to argue the importance and value of including the recognition of dilemma in our teaching and learning programmes, in counselling and in the general entitlement for all students; it also aims to show the feasibility of doing this within current constraints. It will offer suggestions on the different ways in which this may be done by teacher, tutor or counsellor and in the next Chapter attempts to provide a basic justification for this from the philosophy of education.

It must be admitted that there are some almost insuperable problems for the would-be curriculum innovator. Among the many hurdles to leap are public examinations, which at first sight appear to determine and constrict the syllabus; there is a kind of curriculum congestion charge that all teachers have to pay (what is going to be dropped to find room for a new idea?); then there is the perennial difficulty of finding the human and material resources that may be needed. As almost any secondary teacher will confirm, educational ideas may be all very well in themselves and have professional support in detached discussion, but they have no hope of implementation unless first they are required by the examination system, then space can be found in an already overcrowded curriculum, and finally they are adequately funded and staffed. Without these prerequisites being in place, innovative ideas, however reasonable and justified, are doomed to be buried in that great mortuary in the sky containing so much curriculum development of the past century.

This has been true for many decades and a current observation from Thomson (2017), an experienced A level teacher and successful college Principal shows that matters have only worsened in recent years:

> I was probably towards one end of the spectrum of motivation … in taking an ethical position on wanting to do the best for the students we served. More frequently the pragmatic concern about Ofsted provides college leaders with the impetus.
>
> What follows from it I think is a kind of vicious circle; school and college leaders apply pressure on teachers to improve results. Teachers therefore prepare students for the exam through minute scrutiny of and attention to the assessment objectives. They also scrutinise the marking of students' scripts. To safeguard themselves from litigation exam boards insist their markers apply the assessment criteria scrupulously and uniformly. So now boards, teachers and students are all focusing on meeting the assessment objectives. Shakespeare or Cromwell or French grammar or the alkali metals are no longer the primary concern, using these judiciously to obtain a high grade is. This is worse than education being made instrumental; it's actually about supplanting education with assessment as the most important purpose. (Correspondence, 7 June, 2017)

The obstacles are many: it may well be the case that reform has been invariably driven by public examinations, which in turn have usually been dictated by the requirements of universities or employers; it is also undeniable that there is always the practical issue of finding space in the curriculum and getting the necessary staffing and funding to implement change. Furthermore, it is a sad fact that without the motivation of self-interest, for both staff and students, innovations are often just so much vapid idealism. Very few schools and colleges have succeeded in escaping these limitations in the past 100 years, so it is reasonable to ask, what point is there in introducing a new idea now? What spark can be provided to light a new fire?

Nevertheless, we should not despair; there are grounds for optimism. This book is predicated on the belief that it is feasible in practice to include dilemma thinking within current constraints. In the first place, teachers are well aware that their "profession" would be doomed as such, if they were merely puppets of the national system, whether examination syllabuses or government requirements. They do not relish, any more than any other professional, being fixed operatives on a production line required to deliver only what the authorities decide. As the evidence here shows, teachers will readily respond to the opportunity to apply experimental ideas to their teaching and learning, provided that they can see an advantage to the students, or themselves, and that they can in practice be implemented.

Moreover, and crucially, the argument in this chapter is for a paradigm shift in perspective, not the addition of new materials, a change of approach not more content for an already crammed syllabus. That said, let us see what place dilemma thinking could have in the curriculum.

There are three main sources upon which this chapter draws: first, the informal discussions which took place over two years with a group of ten subject tutors in a Sixth Form College, on the recognition and resolution of dilemma (abbreviated to RD). Second, a study visit to the USA to look at a variety of programmes for the "Gifted and Talented" pupils, on critical thinking and problem solving, in a range of schools; these included acceleration, enrichment and "pull out" programmes. Third, a letter and questionnaire which was sent to sixty Heads of Departments in ten different post sixteen institutions across the country, requesting examples and comments on subject specific dilemmas. Drawing on this data, some conclusions and recommendations for tutors and counsellors in post 16 colleges are tentatively put forward.

DILEMMA RESEARCH GROUP

A team of ten volunteer staff was gathered and they began by setting themselves the task of clarifying and refining the meaning of dilemma and the definition in respect of their own subjects. There was no disagreement about a working definition of dilemma, which was accepted as a situation or issue which invited "various approaches, interpretations, strategies or techniques" and therefore had "alternative legitimate solutions". It was also agreed that dilemmas would usually (but not necessarily) have a remainder in the form of a cost such as regret or guilt over the rejected alternative. It was accepted as a working assumption that the recognition of dilemma might vary from one subject to another and therefore the group should draw its membership from across the curriculum.

The following subject disciplines were represented: chemistry, government and politics, geography, design and technology, French, psychology, physical education, classics, physics and religious studies. Meetings took place three or four times a term, after college. There were two weekend study sessions and two pieces of fieldwork amongst students.

Among the questions considered by this group over a period of two years were: Are dilemmas considered to be a part of the course in different subject disciplines and, if so, to what extent are they distinct? What kinds of opportunity occur in post 16 courses to develop the ability to recognize and resolve dilemma? What do different disciplines understand by dilemma?

The expression "recognition of dilemma" (or RD) is frequently used in this study and may need some explanation. It refers to two very different abilities, the first being to perceive the existence of an alternative and the second being to accept its validity. "Recognition" implies not only awareness but also taking cognisance of, "the action of acknowledging as true, valid or entitled to consideration" (Shorter Oxford English Dictionary). It can therefore be said to have these two components:

a. Knowledge, or the awareness that there exist alternative perspectives and different choices to be made. This is simply a recognition of reality in the sense that different people do as a matter of fact hold different opinions on the same issues.
b. Acceptance, or the acknowledgment that at least some of these points of view are legitimate, valid perspectives, that the dilemma is genuine. This is the force of "entitled to consideration".

It was agreed to begin by looking in a fairly general way at the kind of problems students came across in their A level courses which were open ended and admitted several valid solutions. Each member of the group then presented a paper in turn from the perspective of her/his own subject specialism.

Physics

The physicist began by denying that there were any real dilemmas in his subject until a student had progressed far into the subject (to degree level at least). In his view, genuine dilemmas did not arise as such, in A level courses; there was only ignorance or lack of insight. Even when faced with a difficult choice, for example between methods of measurement, there was always a preferred solution, clear to any student with enough knowledge or understanding. When pressed on this, he allowed that it might be a useful pedagogic technique for the teacher to play a game of pretence, to let the student work under the illusion that a dilemma existed and to refrain from providing the missing ingredients of knowledge or insight. The superior and somewhat patronising implications of this were challenged in the subsequent discussion.

Design and Technology

In design and technology the opposite standpoint was taken. Students, it was claimed, were faced with dilemmas from the outset of their course and at every stage; the example was given of a student who was dismayed at the right-handedness of everyday life and the implements available and who wished to design tools for the left handed. There were always different and equally valid options open. Other members of the group questioned whether the examples given were problems rather than true dilemmas; it was also questioned whether there was any sense of cost or regret in making the choice; was it not simply a question of good, basic thinking as applied to problems of design and technology?

Physical Education

An interesting slant on the discussion was provided by the physical education teacher. The example he gave was that of instant decision-making of the kind, "Do

I pass or kick at goal?" "Do I play a lob or make a passing shot?" These were decisions usually made at high speed in response to an immediate situation. This in turn led to a discussion on whether or not that decision was more of an instinctive, reflex action than a considered reflection. In fact, it was suggested that dilemma thinking in physical situations would probably be a case of fatal hesitation or dither. But most members considered that there had to be some cognitive element in such cases, however physical the skill and however instantaneous the decision. It would therefore, they thought, qualify as a dilemma.

Politics and Government

In politics and government the example was given of a discussion on Proportional Representation (PR). It was held that to devise a system of PR would simply constitute a problem, because there was an accepted definition of PR and the task was defined and limited. On the other hand, to consider whether or not one ought to have PR would be a dilemma. The main challenge to this opinion was on the grounds that there was no sense of loss in the rejected alternative. This raised the question whether the existence of a remainder was a sufficient but not a necessary characteristic of dilemma. On this point the group was divided, but most members believed a sense of cost was an essential part of the definition.

Classics

In classics the question was considered, "What life style was enjoyed by Plautus?" (a Roman Playwright of the Old Latin period, said to have worked as a scene shifter and later a manual labourer). This required the student to enter into the life of slaves, and also to express a personal judgment. Able students, it was suggested, might avoid giving any opinion, preferring the safer option of learning, then describing the way of life. This was likened to a swimmer who refused to let go of the side and launch out for fear of making a mistake. This teacher considered "letting go of the side" the most important ability in the recognition of dilemma and to develop the confidence to risk error, even to do badly on occasion.

Religious Studies

When religious studies was considered, a number of dilemmatic questions emerged of the type, "Can there be a Just War in a nuclear age?" This led to such questions as: what value should be placed upon idealism in comparison to practicality? Is religion world affirming or world denying, assuming a pessimistic or an optimistic view of human nature? A more distinctive dilemma was the question of the place of RS in the curriculum; was it an essential part of the culture (as Buddhism might be in Sri Lanka, Catholicism in Spain or Islam in Iran)? If so, who was qualified to teach it, a convinced believer only, or any qualified teacher? The answer clearly would depend upon whether the objectives of RS included, or specifically excluded proselytism. This in turn raised dilemmas for educators and students alike, as both would need to ask to what extent it was permissible (or essential perhaps) to let one's personal standpoints influence the direction of the course.

Modern Languages

In modern languages, it was suggested that the quintessential dilemma was the search for an appropriate translation and the appreciation of meaning. It was also argued that "dilemma for 16–19 year old linguists is the recognition of the need to think in the language and to understand what that actually means; for example, the first positive sign is often dreaming in the language. Not knowing what is coming next is part of this, in that you are not planning the sentence ahead before deciding to speak".

One positive and major outcome of these discussions over the two years was the quality of the contributions, which it was unanimously agreed had a beneficial influence on day-to-day teaching strategies. The vigorous debates which took place not only refined the definition of dilemma but also increased participants' understanding of it in each subject specialism and how it might be included in the college curriculum. After the individual presentations, hypotheses were drawn up to compare the ability to recognize and resolve dilemmas (RD) between "able" students and other students. An assessment procedure and marking scheme was devised and interviews and essays were arranged.

It remained an unresolved question whether dilemma was subject specific or, rather, whether there were subject based perspectives on each dilemma. The outcomes about the chosen hypotheses were (predictably) inconclusive, but as far as the study of dilemma thinking was concerned, they were very encouraging. Dilemmas, as defined, certainly existed in A level courses, as well as general education programmes; it was considered by all, with one exception, to be an important component of good teaching; it was subject specific not in the sense of being a distinct form of knowledge but in the sense that students might be able at recognizing dilemmas in one subject but not in another, or alternatively in college courses but not in their personal lives (and vice versa); it was agreed that RD could be taught and included in the curriculum, preferably within existing courses rather than by arranging a special place for it on the timetable.

A STUDY VISIT TO THE USA

A study visit to the U.S.A was arranged; the purpose was to look at both selective and normal schools and seek educational programmes which might relate to dilemma thinking. The itinerary covered six stays: in New York, where visits were arranged to schools in Harlem, Manhattan and Long Island; then to Princeton, where, in addition to the High School and University, there was an opportunity to learn at first hand from the staff at the Education Testing Service about the thinking behind the Standard Achievement Tests (SAT's) and the Advanced Placement (AP) courses and to what extent dilemmas were included or valued in these. The next visit was to Baltimore to see a renowned School for the Arts, followed by a visit to a School for Technology in Virginia; then to Houston University and the centre for Gifted and Talented Education at the School of Education. The final visit was to San Francisco and look at Gifted and Talented (GT) programmes.

Acceleration, Problem Solving and Fast Thinking

In the US there has been a strong tradition of teaching critical thinking and selective schools, for example in New York, fought hard against the prevailing educational policy in order to remain selective. In that situation, the main policy for teaching the "gifted and talented", or very able students, as well as those with special needs, has been concerned with finding answers to defined and closed questions; a high premium is placed on problem solving and fast thinking.

Typical of this fashion is the attitude of the Head, in one such school, which included two Nobel prize-winners amongst the recent alumni, who commented to me that, "provided you have the genetic basis, what you need to motivate a pupil is economic striving"; he put success down to diversity, challenging teaching, questioning, and out of class activities such as publications, plays and concerts.

It was hard to find any acknowledgment that dilemmas existed, at least in academic situations. Problems had solutions and reaching conclusions at speed was rewarded, together with confident and articulate argument and competitive activity. As a result, the preferred and most successful approach towards their most able students was to accelerate them in specific subjects.

Enrichment Programmes

Another approach was "enrichment". On Long Island I was able to visit a special centre for Gifted Programmes, starting at the third grade. The state had provided some funding for salaries, materials, software and a coordinator. Parents, too, were very supportive. Each Middle School had a teacher servicing three classes and on a rota basis the pupils selected (according to a multi-criteria definition) were "pulled out" and bussed to the centre in order to receive enrichment sessions for three hours a week.

The activities were varied, clearly enjoyed by the eight and nine-year olds, and noisy, with plenty of visual material. Written on the board was a quotation purported to be from Einstein, "The soul never thinks without an image". The theoretical backbone was Bloom's taxonomy (even to the children they spoke of "meta-cognition", "synthesis" and "problem solving") and the staff consciously aimed at the higher order thinking. Fast responses were encouraged but there was not the same stress on "correct" answers as at the selective schools previously visited. One activity was called "Alike it or not", in which the teacher presented the pupils with a set of four words, numbers or pictures and asked them to put their thumbs up or down to indicate whether they saw a likeness; it was suggested that one would be the odd one out (for example, dime, rope, glass, slide; foot, hand, knee, cheek; 127 52 108 99). The aim was to loosen up the rigid mind and to create confidence in their own thinking. As long as they could justify the similarity, there was no search for a "correct solution".

Also relevant to the understanding of dilemma thinking were the programmes undertaken at a School for Technology in Virginia. Here 85% of the pupils were already identified as Gifted and Talented. Admission was competitive and although they tried to meet some ethnic and gender quotas, the tests were strict; 20% screening was provided by a maths, verbal, spatial and abstract reasoning test. This was followed by an essay to discover motivation. In the classes, the participation was impressive. A conscious effort was made to promote divergent thinking, discussion and argument.

Once again, I found that the preferred strategy for the most gifted was acceleration, although not to the exclusion of enrichment, because most staff considered their teaching was already "enriched". Three students were already attending Princeton University for mathematics lectures, whilst still on the school roll. In this way, they retained their pastoral and social links with their known age group. Within the school there was considerable counselling before pupils were accelerated to a senior class.

At the Center for GT Education at Houston University, there were 40 teachers doing an MA on GT education (fifteen other similar set-ups existed in other universities in the USA at that time). Much work was being done on how to teach problem solving and critical thinking, but I could find nothing that encouraged the recognition or resolution of dilemma (or anything like it).

Outside San Francisco, one school had recently been identified as one of the "top ten" schools in the USA and was the only school in San Francisco to be selective (indeed only one other state funded selective school existed at this time throughout California). Scores for SAT' would be in the top 15% and there were many considered gifted; these were placed on an accelerated track in a specific subject after counselling. The Principal strongly denied it was an elitist school. "True elitism occurs only when there is an economic or social advantage obtained, not when it occurs by merit", he said. He preferred breadth to accelerated advance and personally encouraged creative and divergent thinking in the school.

Most administrators met on this visit were eclectic in their approach to the identification and teaching of the "Gifted and Talented", using both enrichment and acceleration strategies for their most able pupils. Segregation in the form of "Pull out" programmes and special schools was a more controversial policy and in many districts was ruled out on political or social grounds. In the best examples witnessed, students were encouraged to think divergently, creatively and to allow for alternative approaches. They were also encouraged to be confident of their own ideas and to practise articulating them.

Specially funded programmes, however, with specific objectives along such lines were confined to those pupils identified as gifted and talented. A strong impression was gained, throughout the visit, that most G and T pupils on special programmes were taught that problems have correct solutions and that there is a right answer to be sought by the brightest minds in the shortest possible time.

A SURVEY OF HEADS OF DEPARTMENT

This study visit was then followed up by an enquiry amongst 60 Heads of Departments in post sixteen institutions in the UK. The earlier small-scale study referred to above had given considerable encouragement to expect that many teachers would think that dilemmatic issues were an important part of their specific subjects. To follow this up a letter was sent to 60 Heads of Department in ten different post sixteen institutions. Dilemma was defined as "a situation in which a choice has to be made between at least two pressing alternatives, where there is no obvious solution" and examples were given of both moral and non-moral issues. It was explained that the research interest was to discover "the extent to which there are opportunities to "practise" this common predicament in college based examination courses (i.e. not simply in general courses or tutor periods)". A questionnaire was enclosed.

The first surprise was the response, which was very encouraging; 43 (72%) replied which was a considerably higher percentage than was expected. Many were positive, even enthusiastic about the matter, enclosing photocopies of parts of the syllabus they taught, adding a page of explanatory notes, in order to elaborate on their ideas. In one case, five pages of closely argued analysis of texts, ranging from the Book of Job to Hamlet, illustrated dilemmas of the intellect and of the soul, the mental process from confusion to enlightenment, via various levels of realisation, agony and "eureka" type discovery to occasional resolution. One said the questionnaire had jogged him into the realisation of the importance of the subject and several wished to be kept informed of any findings or outcome. In all, 19 different subjects were represented by the respondents. All, with one exception, acknowledged the existence of dilemmas in their subjects although one wrote that "they should be avoided if possible by careful planning". The exception thought it unprofitable for students to consider the question of dilemma, because it could only lead to confusion in a student's mind!

Amongst the respondents, 38% said they covered the issue weekly and only 2 (3%) said that they never considered the matter. One was a biologist (while four other biologists gave several examples from their teaching and said it was "very worthwhile"); the other was a mathematician (which did not agree with the view of another mathematician who claimed to deal with dilemmas regularly).

When asked what value they would personally place on the consideration of "dilemma" type problems in a student's general education, all except one thought it "worthwhile" (33% said "very worthwhile"). A similar figure thought such problems in vocational education to be worthwhile (15%), very worthwhile (33%). Despite the high proportion who thought it worthwhile or very worthwhile and who considered dilemmas frequently, nearly half of the respondents could not recall having had any teacher training or preparation in the recognition of resolution of dilemma; even so, there was a substantial number who considered dilemmas frequently in their main course; 38% said this was weekly, 7% monthly, 18% occasionally and only two respondents said that they never considered the question at all.

They all were asked to give examples of the type of dilemma which students considered as part of the course. It was suggested that this might perhaps be "a set assignment, an essay topic, part of the coursework, a practical or experiment". The replies covered a wide range of topics and problems, providing evidence that moral issues occur in every discipline, particularly in its application.

There was manifestly no shortage of examples of the type:

- Which type of energy production should a developing country spend its scarce resources on developing? (geography)
- Siting a chemical plant (chemistry)
- Funding the Health Service, how to allocate scarce resources (sociology)
- Government economic policy – the need to raise revenue while preserving an image as the party of low taxation (government and politics)
- The morality of feeding grain to cattle in the rich world whilst approx one billion starve (geography)

Some illustrated a general concern for the study skills and stressful choices that students could sometimes face:

- Do I miss lessons to make deadlines or not?
- Students preparing a group demonstration are faced with maintaining their individuality (by stressing their own ideas) or accepting the dominance of others, so benefiting the group's progress. (theatre studies)
- A key stage is when a piece of work is nearly finished when it is frequently possible for the artist to do something that will either brilliantly resolve a piece or ruin it. (Art and Design)
- Dealing with young children who exhibit behaviour difficult to handle. (health education)

It was sometimes difficult to see just how subject specific some dilemmas were. For example:

- Revolutionaries in nineteenth century Tsarist Russia – what methods to use to effect change, propaganda or assassination? (history)
- The dilemma of GDR citizens in 1989, go West for jobs but leave family, friends and home behind. (German)
- Whether to seek full employment or to reduce inflation. (economics)
- Students are presented data about the candidate drugs and they are asked to recommend one of the drugs for further development. (chemistry)
- The impact of science on military decisions. (physics)

How much German is required to deal with the GDR immigrant problem and how much chemistry is required to locate a chemical plant, or PH to assess the impact of science on military strategy? Arguably very little, and the subject knowledge is therefore separable from the dilemma. What this reveals is that there are no English dilemmas or chemistry dilemmas as such, but rather issues which can be diagnosed and perceived from a particular discipline but not confined within it. On the other hand, a decision as to which chemical to develop cannot be taken without scientific knowledge; some understanding of economics is needed to allocate scarce resources and knowledge of history is desirable before discussing the choices confronting Tsarist revolutionaries.

It is worth noting, in passing, that the question, "Are there any dilemmas in your subject?" is not the same as; "Are there any distinctively physics type dilemmas?" The former can legitimately include applied moral issues, of the type "Is it right to build a nuclear reactor on that site?" In the same way, students studying German might properly be asked to look at current historical or cultural issues and thereby face a question about GDR emigrants. But, however valid these situations might be as dilemmas, none of them substantiates the proposition that there are subject specific dilemmas. This possibly would explain why one of the scientists claimed that there are no specifically scientific dilemmas as such, only dilemmas of application. It should be noted that these may lead to collaborations between different subject teachers and in turn to different perspectives and more complex discussions.

A parallel and well-known problem is where to locate moral education, given that moral education is not a distinct discipline (as opposed to moral philosophy). Should it be taught within other disciplines or as a separate subject? Similarly, "Can study skills be acquired apart from particular studies?" The answer given by most teachers is of a "both-and" nature rather than "either-or". As in moral education, there are formal characteristics or skills of argument and organisation, theory and concept where all the possible exemplars will come from other disciplines and cannot effectively be studied apart from them. The same argument applies to teaching the recognition of dilemma.

THE ROLE OF THE COUNSELLOR

Student counselling has developed greatly in the last fifty years. Prior to that counselling was undertaken by chaplains, and by the one to one relationship offered by tutors. The pastoral side of a tutor's role, giving individual advice and assistance, has long been a distinct feature in European education. Today, there are numerous training schemes and courses and, although the first American course in counsellor education was offered by Harvard University in the summer of 1911, the impact of the new discipline of counselling and guidance did not make a significant impact upon further and Higher education in the UK until the 1960's. By 1973 the Association for Student Counselling had almost 200 members; by 1992 membership had risen to 552. Today by far the majority of Universities and Further Education colleges in the UK have the services at least of a part-time counsellor.

Counsellors deal with the given. They are trained not to let their preconceptions intrude into the needs of their clients. It is one thing to hold an opinion on the existence of dilemmas; it is quite another to counsel students who perceive themselves in the middle of one. In theory, their choices of attitude might be: either dilemmas do not really exist or there is no need to accommodate them for they are merely problems awaiting a solution. Or dilemmas do exist, but they are mistaken perceptions and there is a need to re-educate the student to see things correctly. Or they do exist and there is a need to counsel the regret and remorse or guilt. Or they do exist and are to be welcomed.

Thus, it ought to be of little consequence whether or not individual counsellors personally believe in the existence of genuine dilemmas. Students, as a matter of fact, experience dilemmas on a daily basis; some are deeply troubled and distressed by them. The tutor or counsellor is there to provide support in such situations. She or he might wish to persuade students to cut through the problem, to clarify it, to reach a reasonable solution, or they might wish to show how dilemmas are a universal experience, and living with them is an inevitable part of adult life.

Late Adolescence – A Distinctive Period

As tutors and counsellors would attest, late adolescence is a particularly interesting period of development. Several studies (e.g., Marcia, 1980; Erikson, 1968) reveal 16–19 year olds to be a distinct group, on the threshold of adulthood. Louizos in a study of sixth form college students "confirmed late adolescence as a distinct phase in the life cycle, qualitatively different to the earlier teenage years ... Lessons have been learned from it and incorporated into new structures and strategies for dealing with life" (1994, p. 54).

Writers have described this period variously as a time of "turmoil" (Offer, 1969), the "doldrums" (Winnicott, 1968), a "normative crisis" (Erikson, 1968). Noonan (1983) specifically likens this whole period to living in a permanent dilemma:

> The active and emotionally energetic process of mourning provides a model for the adolescence transition, since both are attempts to achieve a sense of personal continuity out of the confusion of drastic disruption ... It is easiest to see and describe the mourning process when the loss is stark, when someone actually dies and cannot be retrieved in any physical way. The survivor is faced with a dilemma: of letting the dead person go while still giving him space in life as a living if not palpable being ... (1983, p. 3)

> We can sometimes feel that our childhood has been irretrievably lost. For instance, we can return to our family, home and childhood haunts and relationships, but they will never be as they were when we left them, because we and they have done things in the meantime ... Personal maturation requires some things to be yielded to make way for new ones; it requires us to convert childhood into a memory which is alive, if not palpable, inside us, and this

means we have to mourn aspects of our child-self so they may be internalised. (1983, p. 5)

As late adolescents, students are acquiring independence from parents, from society, from each other, in an effort to gain "identity status" which according to Erikson (1968) means "the accrued confidence that one's ability to maintain inner sameness and continuity (one's ego in the psychological sense) is matched by the sameness and continuity of one's meaning for others" (1968, p. 159).

Marcia (1966) developed Erikson's concept of "identity" and provided a specific model of "ego identity", offering a precise analysis. Bilsker (1992) adapted these ideas through the eyes of an existentialist and stressed the freedom of individual choice which each adolescent has in breaking away from previous constraints. Certainly, the interviews with students revealed a sense of freedom, rather than a sense of being imprisoned and determined.

Students have difficulties peculiar to their age group. There are several lists of such problems. Lago and Shipton (1994) provide a summary which includes: relationship difficulties, with parents and other family members, "learning how to get into intimate relationships, but just as importantly, how to leave them is a major concern"; academic difficulties, impaired performance (study skills, writing or presentation), exam problems, loss of motivation (apathy) and failure with its aftermath; there are emotional and psychological problems, a wide category which "covers all kinds of anxiety, depression, eating disorders, adjustment to loss and bereavement, self image; self-defeating patterns of behaviour, obsessional thinking; and also fears and stresses caused by ill health or disability" (pp. 27–34). They also list problems linked to transitions, homesickness and new academic demands.

Louizos found that students rarely admitted to having problems: "Most students claimed to have few problems and even fewer serious ones" (1994, p. 44). There was a general reluctance to disclose based on the fear of not being understood and of getting too close to others. The need to feel "really understood" governed the choice of confidant(e), whether friend, parent or counsellor. The most common coping strategy was found to be self-reliance "as only oneself can truly understand". The importance of privacy and resistance to intrusion was confirmed by the evidence.

The danger of using category lists of problems is that this "predetermines the options in how a problem might be defined" (Lago & Shipton, 1994, p. 27). Nor do they help our investigation beyond alerting counsellors and tutors to the kinds of issue which might form the raw material of a dilemma. Whatever school or training (and it is not part of this study to evaluate counselling theory) the counsellor will be working with tutors and supporting them. Their role is also changing. Tutors in post 16 colleges today occupy not only an adult role model but also operate as friend, a peculiarly difficult half-way position in which to operate; they are the professional expert and facilitator but also, they are seen to be just the other side of the fully adult threshold.

Perhaps the most important conclusion, as far as the counsellor is concerned, is that students do experience dilemmas, as well as problems and that they are quite capable of distinguishing between the two; that, nevertheless, they are reluctant to admit to either; that they wish to be self reliant and to resolve them if possible without help, and so avoid relapsing into a form of dependency from which they are, as young adults, just emerging; above all, that they need to be able to face the uncertainties and ambiguities implied by dilemma, the post decisional conflicts, the doubts, regrets and occasionally the guilt which they carry with them afterwards. Reflective common sense is likely to be their only aid. Standing by to listen when invited, responding without "giving the answers" or removing from the students their ownership of the decision, is probably the most valuable role that the counsellor and tutor can fulfil.

This completes our look at some of the evidence from practitioners in High Schools in the USA and UK Secondary Schools. It will be useful now to discuss whether there is an underlying educational or philosophical theory to which one can turn to support the case being made for enriching the curriculum with a greater appreciation of dilemma.

HOW AWARENESS OF DILEMMA CAN ENRICH EDUCATION

Seeking a Philosophical Rationale

Key Points

- On being open minded
- The experience of conflict
- Philosophy should not prescribe
- A liberal education
- Objections to a liberal education
- Teachers and dilemmatic spaces

ON BEING OPEN MINDED

Can a rationale be found for including the understanding of dilemma in our schools and colleges? One place to start is in Dewey's theory of education, which has seen something of a revival of interest in recent years. In his work on *How We Think*, originally written in 1910 but extensively revised in 1933, he writes of the desirability of being open minded, which means to

> Include an active desire to listen to more sides than one, to give heed to facts from whatever source they come, to give full attention to alternative possibilities, to recognize the possibility of error even in the beliefs that are dearest to us. (Dewey, 1933, p. 30)

Giving full attention to alternative possibilities supports the case for students learning to recognize dilemma, where it occurs, in all their subjects. Similarly, an interesting slant on the case for leaving questions open, in order to avoid the "pitfalls of Answerland", can be found in the work of Russell and Bullock (1999). Reporting on the exchange of emails between them as educator and student teacher Bullock writes:

> As a student teacher I found … that I am reminded of unresolved issues that I would like to explore in the future … There are many issues that cannot be "answered". Instead they must be constantly revisited …

© KONINKLIJKE BRILL NV, LEIDEN, 2018 | DOI 9789004368118_004

Tom [the educator] was adept at not giving "the right answer" on issues and opinions that I raised via electronic mail. Instead he would ask more questions to help me reflect on a deeper level and get to the heart of the matter. I now realize he was avoiding the pitfalls associated with what our physics methods class came to all Answerland – the near universal tendency of teachers and students to focus on the pursuit of right answers ... The questions Tom asked always pointed me towards deeper meanings. (Loughran, 1999, p. 135ff)

This echoes well the views of Postman and Weingarten (1971):

The new education has as its purpose the development of a new kind of person, one who ... is an actively inquiring, flexible, creative, innovative, tolerant, liberal personality, who can face uncertainty and ambiguity without disorientation. (p. 204)

THE EXPERIENCE OF CONFLICT

Perhaps the most powerful justification for the consideration of dilemma in a person's education is to be found in Nussbaum. She bases her argument on the practical conflicts in Greek tragedy, especially the slaughter of Iphigenia by Agamemnon (1985):

I must now add, with the Agamemnon Chorus, that the experience of conflict can also be a time of learning and development ... hard cases like these, if one allows oneself really to see and to experience them, may bring progress along with their sorrow, a progress that comes from an increase in self-knowledge and knowledge of the world. An honest effort to do justice to all aspects of a hard case, seeing and feeling it in all its conflicting many-sidedness, could enrich future deliberative efforts. Through the experience of choice, Eteocles might have discovered cares to which justice had not previously been done; Agamemnon might have come to a new understanding of piety and of the love he owes his family. (p. 260)

It is a regrettable fact of experience that it often takes the shock of suffering pain to learn many of the values of human relationships, to discover self-knowledge and to make us examine our lives afresh. It would be inconceivable to plan this as part of the curriculum. We must, therefore, take seriously Illich's (1973) observations that "most learning happens casually" (p. 20) that "we have all learned most of what we know outside school. Everyone learns how to live outside school. We learn to speak, to think, to love, to feel, to play, to curse, to politick and to work without interference from a teacher" (p. 35). This undervalues the part of reflection and the opportunities to reflect, to reason and to be guided in forming a balanced judgment occur predominantly within schools and colleges. Taken with Nussbaum's remarks, this is the fundamental justification for considering both the recognition and resolution of dilemmas during adolescent educational experience.

PHILOSOPHY SHOULD NOT PRESCRIBE

On the other hand, the question remains, can a philosophical rationale for including dilemma in the curriculum be found? It is a deceptively simple question because it suggests that it is somehow the business of philosophers to prescribe the content or method in education and, moreover, that if and when this is done, there is a consensus that may be treated as a *vade mecum* for the guidance of educators.

We have seen grounds for thinking that a majority of teachers believe that there is indeed a place for including dilemmas in the post sixteen curriculum. Many would no doubt call these "philosophical", perhaps linking them with the tradition of "liberal education" in this Western Europe. But the picture is no clearer when we look at modern liberal democracies. The idea that educators might discover some agreed guide, theoretical basis or common practice on which to base their policies is fruitless. As long ago as 1950 Jeffreys remarked, with more than a touch of romantic nostalgia:

> The most serious weakness in modern education is the uncertainty about its aims. A glance over history reminds that the most vital and effective systems of education have envisaged their objectives quite definitely, in terms of personal qualities and social situations. Spartan, Feudal, Jesuit, Nazi, Communist educations have had this in common; they knew what they wanted to do and believed in it. By contrast, education in the liberal democracies is distressingly nebulous in its aims. (p. 61)

On the question of an agreed consensus, we can see over the centuries that this has never existed in practice. Aristotle (1962) expressed his uncertainty like this:

> We must not leave out of sight the nature of education and the proper means of imparting it. For at present there is a practical dissension on this point; people do not agree on the subjects which the young should learn, whether they take virtue in the abstract or the best life as the end to be sought, and it is uncertain whether education should be properly directed rather to the cultivation of the intellect or the moral discipline. The question is complicated, too, if we look at the actual education of our own day; nobody knows whether the young should be trained at such studies as are merely useful as means of livelihood or in such as tend to the promotion of virtue or in the higher studies, all of which have received a certain number of suffrages. Nor again, if virtue be accepted as the end, is there any agreement as to the means of attaining it. (7.2.13337a33)

In contrast, O'Hear (1981) had no doubt that philosophy could provide a supportive rationale:

> One's philosophy of education ... will be distinct from a sociology of education; reflecting one's values and concept of what men (sic) ought to be, as opposed to what they might be in any particular society. It also ... reflects one's ideals for society as a whole. In saying that a philosophy of education reflects one's

concept of what men ought to be, it can be distinguished from a psychology of education. Human nature is not something that is just given. It is something we can make something of, in the light of how we conceive ourselves and others ... So a philosophy of education will attempt to specify a set of educational aims, justifying them in the light of our general ethical values. (p. 1)

On the other hand, Peters (1973) doubted if was sensible to ask about the aims of education. He found it an odd philosophical question. In his view, at best it served as a "salutary request for teachers to survey what they are doing, get their priorities straight, concentrate their attention on them, and discard irrelevancies" (p. 14). He would have us concentrate on worthwhile activities, implied by the meaning of the word "education" itself and leave aside thoughts of distant goals:

To be educated is not to have arrived at a destination; it is to travel with a different view. What is required is not feverish preparation for something that lies ahead, but to work with precision, passion, and taste at worthwhile things that lie to hand. (1965, p. 110)

Thus Peters (1964) undercut the search for a philosophical rationale by denying what he called the "layman's view that the task of the philosopher is to provide some kind of synoptic directive for living" (p. 8). Approaching the question of educational aims from the analytic tradition, he argued that the word 'education' like 'reform' had a norm built into it, which "functions as a very distant target for such activities ... 'Education', like 'reform' picks out a family of processes culminating in a person being better" (1973, p. 15).

Whilst this view has been strongly challenged (e.g., by Woods & Dray, 1973), it can safely be concluded that unless one can find a prior argument for saying that recognizing and resolving dilemmas is a "worthwhile" activity in itself, and being adept at it is to be a better person, philosophy will not provide one. Perhaps, as Vernon (1942) said of the place of psychology in education, philosophy has a lowlier role to play:

Educational psychology is in many respects an advanced and highly technical form of applied science. Owing to the nature of the material with which it deals, it is more comparable to medicine than, say, to physical engineering; it cannot by itself give answers to definite questions about the art of teaching. Still less can it affirm the soundness of educational policies or ideals; perhaps it is more often useful in a negative way, that is to say in indicating what principles are unsound. (p. 99)

A LIBERAL EDUCATION

A different line of argument can be developed based on the idea of a liberal education. The consideration of moral values (and dilemmas amongst them) together with the ideas of generality and breadth are often attributed to this tradition, which is central to the educational practices and institutions of most western countries, at least until recently. O'Hear (1973) describes a liberal education as consisting in:

Initiating students into disciplines such as those of mathematics, science, history literature and the arts. ... Students are to be taught by teachers who have some claim to authority in what they teach ... All involved ... are to be guided by the standards of excellence inherent in the disciplines concerned, wherever these standards might lead, even into conflict with church or state ... it is not primarily vocational or practical. (p. 4)

Recognising that a liberal education is a process concerned directly with the pursuit of knowledge, Hirst (1973) defines education in terms of "man's knowledge of what is the case". As knowledge is itself a distinctive human virtue, "liberal education has a value for the person as the fulfilment of the mind, a value which has nothing to do with utilitarian or vocational considerations" (p. 88). This inevitably involves a consideration of values, the source of which, Hirst argued, cannot be found in religious, political or utilitarian theories; these are always open to debate and doubt. He sought a more "ultimate basis for the values that should determine education, some more objective ground". This, Hirst claimed, is discovered if one ensures that knowledge corresponds to objective reality. "A liberal education in the pursuit of knowledge is, therefore, seeking the development of the mind according to what is quite external to it, the structure and pattern of reality" (p. 90). From this position Hirst developed his argument for there being discrete forms of knowledge, which he summarised as follows:

(I) Distinct disciplines or forms of knowledge (subdivisible: mathematics, physical sciences, human sciences, history, religion, literature and the fine arts, philosophy).

(II) Fields of knowledge: theoretical, practical (these may or may not include elements of moral knowledge). It is the distinct disciplines that basically constitute the range of unique ways we have of understanding experience if to these is added moral knowledge. (p. 105)

The subsequent debate led many practitioners to identify Hirst's "forms of knowledge" with a list of subject disciplines (something he was reluctant to do) and thereby to derive a school curriculum. The conclusion of this argument is that the consideration of dilemma would find a place within the "moral knowledge", which is rather untidily "added" to the other forms of knowledge.

Since Hirst's attempt to categorise objective knowledge, in order to find a sound basis for a liberal education, there have been many other attempts to subdivide the elements required in a satisfactory curriculum. Phenix (1964), who proposed six "Realms of Meaning" which were characteristically "human", argued that:

The highest good to be served by education is the fullest possible realization of the distinctively human capacities and that these capacities consist in the life of

51

meaning. Hence the course of study should be such as to maximize meanings. (p. 267)

Amongst other attempts may be mentioned the H.M.I. Report (1977) which argued pragmatically for eight "Areas of Experience" (p. 30). Since then there have been increasingly utilitarian attempts to hijack the curriculum in order to serve technological or industrial or social purposes. What, for the purposes of this study, is significant is that there is in practice no difficulty in locating the consideration of dilemmas within the curriculum, although it would be hard to justify it as a distinct "Form of Knowledge", "Realm of Meaning" or "Area of Experience".

OBJECTIONS TO A LIBERAL EDUCATION

A number of objections to a "liberal education" have been voiced. O'Hear (1981) identifies five: first, it is sometimes said to be unnatural. The liberal intellectual becomes cut off from his natural roots. His education is contrasted sharply and critically with a natural peasant life, one of simplicity, self-sufficiency, manual work, closeness to nature, fraternity, honour and hospitality. The intellectual may be clever but he is not wise. This idealistic picture of an education which corrupts innocent children is associated with the writings of Tolstoy and Rousseau.

Second, liberal education can be described as "irreligious", in the sense that it gives priority to worldly and secular distractions which can conflict with religious dogma. A fundamentalist approach to education (O'Hear quotes examples from Protestant groups such as the Amish in North America, some Moslems and some Catholics) will not approve of education taking place in an irreligious (or even neutral) setting and would certainly wish to censor certain topics (such as biological evolution or sexual ethics) from being considered at all. In the same way, a number of families prefer home tuition to taking the perceived risk of exposing their children to such influences as adolescent relationships, drugs, alcohol and other pressures.

Third, a liberal education can be thought of as undemocratic; the teacher, by being regarded as the expert in pursuit of excellence, can easily impose both content and method of learning upon pupils, whose voice and cooperation are essential in a democratic community. Fourth, a number of left wing sociologists have advocated radical reforms in education, even the abandonment of schooling altogether. Fifth, it can be seen as irrelevant to the experience of most participants and should be reformed to be based on the objects and concepts familiar to pupils.

None of these alternative "philosophies" of education affects the need to face up to dilemmas. It will be apparent, however, that totalitarian or fundamentalist doctrines are unsympathetic to any position which allows, even extols, the notion of doubt. It has been said that "the sane man doubts often, the drunkard seldom and the madman never" (origin unknown), but this, whilst welcome in a liberal education born in the religious disputes of the sixteenth and seventeenth centuries and favouring tolerance, would be considered morally feeble and intellectually indecisive in opposing traditions.

O'Hear declares roundly that "what we want to do in schooling is to prepare pupils for adult life", a view which would be endorsed by most practitioners (although it begs the questions that most would want to debate about precise content or method). Therefore, in so far as the case has been established that the experience of dilemmas is a common feature of adult, and indeed adolescent, life, dilemma thinking clearly has an essential place within the curriculum.

When we consider where to locate the study of dilemmas, the same arguments that can be brought against teaching moral education as a separate subject apply equally to the consideration of dilemmas. Whilst moral philosophy, in so far as it has a place in the post sixteen curriculum (and I would want to say that it does), would need to be treated separately, there is a strong case for considering dilemmas, like moral education itself, not in terms of a specific subject but rather as pervading the whole college in all its activities. The moral dimension and dilemma with it, would be considered in each discipline and in every activity, not given a special label and confined to a particular room or spot on the timetable.

CONCLUSION

At the outset of the previous chapter, attention was drawn to the near insuperable obstacles to any curriculum development ideas being implemented: the examination system, the time constraints and a lack of human and financial resources. I hope that each of these has been addressed and neutralised, if not removed. We do not need to wait for examinations to include specific references to dilemma thinking. Awareness of dilemmas (RD) can only lead to a deeper understanding of questions set, whether in examinations themselves or in the courses leading to them; furthermore, there is no need for there to be any resource implication, as long as there is a change of mind-set.

It has been argued that teaching and learning within the framework of a liberal education, means avoiding the closed mind approach of fundamentalists, or that of the wrongly named "biblical education", in order to prepare students with adequate tools for adult life. There can be little doubt that to do this requires the recognition of dilemma to be included as an essential part of pedagogic strategy.

The claim here is that good teaching and learning will automatically develop the skills needed to recognize and resolve dilemmas as part of a realistic preparation for work or higher education. Postman and Weingartner (1971) expressed the outcome well, in terms of "good learners":

Good learners prefer to rely on their own judgement ... Good learners are usually not fearful of being wrong. They recognize their limitations and suffer no trauma in concluding that what they believe is apparently not so. In other words, they can change their mind. Changing the character of their minds is what good learners are most interested in doing … Good learners are emphatically not fast answerers …

Perhaps most importantly, good learners do not need to have an absolute, final irrevocable resolution to every problem. The sentence, "I don't know", does not depress them, and they certainly prefer it to the various forms of semantic nonsense that pass for answers to questions that do not as yet have any solution – or may never have one. (p. 42)

Having considered what might be called the groundwork for our educational edifice, it is time to look at how it applies to the adult world of work, taking as an example posts with public responsibility, political accountability or social influence.

PREPARATION AT SCHOOL FOR PUBLIC RESPONSIBILITY

The "Dirty Hands" Dispute

Key Points

- Public and private morality
- Taking up arms: the pacifist and the expedient arguments
- Machiavelli: compromise and expediency
- Sartre: "dirty hands"
- The dilemma of nuclear deterrence
- A distinctive public morality

PUBLIC AND PRIVATE MORALITY

There must be few roles for which our school years should prepare us, which are more important or challenging than that of holding public office. Although dilemmas occur in every area of human activity, none is more eye catching than the political. Often, they bitterly divide a country, as with the vote for independence in Catalonia, the public protest in London against war in Iraq, or Afghanistan, and the UK referendum on membership of the EU and subsequent Brexit negotiations. Probably every country in every year has at least one acrimonious issue which alienates part of their electorate.

In fact, it would be possible, although I believe erroneous, to claim that every political decision is dilemmatic. Erroneous because most of these issues have a rational solution and, although still acrimonious and the cause of intense resentment and rancour, because people reason differently, they are therefore more of a problem than a dilemma. Consider the most effective response to North Korean threats, whether to impeach a US President, how to resolve the West Bank settlement or worldwide question of refugees: these issues are not insoluble, however intractable and tough they might be; the solution follows from the criteria and the moral code. Agreeing the latter is what defeats governments. It becomes a dilemma rather than a problem when there are two opposing moral codes. For example, what are we to make of it when the moral code that a person acknowledges in a post of public responsibility conflicts with the code that the same person accepts in private life?

© KONINKLIJKE BRILL NV, LEIDEN, 2018 | DOI 9789004368118_005

Take the general who knowingly orders an attack on a village with innocent civilians in it, on the pretext that it also contains guerrillas; does he act according to a different set of precepts from those he would normally follow as a private citizen? Are politicians who obtain office by means of a shady deal with an influential pressure group they would normally detest, or who exercise their newly acquired power by compromising the principles for which they stood before winning it, obeying a different moral code? Or are they rather applying the same moral code to a new and more complex situation, adapting the commitments which they would normally acknowledge with more subtlety, complexity and permissible exceptions than would be acceptable in their private lives?

An example in the UK was seen in 2017 when Tim Farron announced his resignation as Liberal Democrat leader after he was repeatedly pressed during the general election over his personal beliefs on issues including homosexuality. Farron issued a statement saying he felt "remaining faithful to Christ" was incompatible with leading his party. He commented:

> From the very first day of my leadership, I have faced questions about my Christian faith. I've tried to answer with grace and patience. Sometimes my answers could have been wiser. The consequences of the focus on my faith is that I have found myself torn between living as a faithful Christian and serving as a political leader.

> To be a political leader – especially of a progressive, liberal party in 2017 – and to live as a committed Christian, to hold faithfully to the Bible's teaching, has felt impossible for me. (*The Guardian*, 14 June, 2017)

This conflict between public and private morality is sometimes called the "dirty hands" problem, after Sartre's play of that name (1955), or the "Machiavellian problem", after the advice given to those seeking high office by Machiavelli in *The Prince* (Chapter XV). Essentially this issue is whether public morality can be considered to differ in some way from private morality, and although usually thought of as a political dilemma, it clearly applies with equal force to military leaders, to those in business management or people in any post of responsibility. The purpose of this chapter is to consider first the variety of situations in which the problem can arise; second, to ask if there is any justification in considering that public life is somehow different from private, and to look at some differing approaches to the problem.

The clash between public and private ethical standpoints is as old as drama and myth. It was essentially the predicament, which Agamemnon faced when he was required to sacrifice his daughter to the gods. Does he follow his duty as the Greek commander, or his duty as a father? A parallel story occurs in the Old Testament when Abraham was tested by God with the command to sacrifice his son and had to decide between his religious and his paternal duty. Early Christian theologians (such as Tertullian, Augustine and Basil the Great) faced the same issue when they debated whether their conscience would allow them to bear arms even when the State decided it was in a just cause.

The first thorough examination came when Machiavelli studied the problem but in recent years, it has been given a new twist in the debate about the rules of war. The potential for mass destruction in modern nuclear warfare has challenged the very notion of there being any such thing as a "just war", and modern investigative journalism has brought into the light of public scrutiny the compromises occurring in modern power politics. Moreover, TV technology now means that the public enters more immediately into the debates surrounding notorious events such as the My Lai massacre in Vietnam, or Watergate. Let us look at some of these arguments in more detail.

TAKING UP ARMS: THE PACIFIST AND THE EXPEDIENT ARGUMENTS

One of the main political compromises faced by the early church was whether Christians could with a clear conscience fight in the Roman army (See Appendix (j)). If so, could they kill without incurring guilt? The two poles of the argument, which might be named the absolutist and the expedient, presented relatively clear positions: either Christians ought to remain pacifist and refuse to enlist even at the point of death or they were justified in obeying the commands of the State ("Be subject for the Lord's sake to every human institution" 1 Peter 2:13), in which case, however regrettable the consequences, no guilt was incurred.

At one extreme stood Tertullian, who can be seen as an early Christian example of the uncompromising absolutist. He rejected the worldly (i.e. Roman) attitude towards war. "It is absolutely forbidden to repay evil with evil" (On Patience 8). "How will a Christian go to war, nay, how will he serve even in peace without a sword, which the Lord has taken away?" (*On Idolatry* XIX). The expedient or compromise position was adopted by his not considering it wrong to kill if the cause was just, although it was the kind of thing that might make a soldier melancholy and sad:

> It is the wrong doing of the opposing party which compels the wise man to wage just wars; and this wrongdoing even though it gave rise to no war, would still be a matter of grief to man because it is man's wrongdoing ... Let everyone, then, who thinks with pain on all these great evils, so horrible, so ruthless, acknowledge that this is misery. And if anyone either endures or thinks of them without mental pain, this is a more miserable plight still, for he thinks himself happy because he has lost human feeling. (*City of God*, XIX.7)

It was right, therefore, to feel melancholy at being compromised by worldly standards; good men should always deprecate war. Guilt, however, was not appropriate. We might parallel this argument with modern versions of expediency; Utilitarians find no place for feelings of guilt if the action is justified in terms of its outcome, although even misplaced guilt may still have its benefits (see Slote, 1985, p. 164). In none of these cases do we have a dilemma as such and therefore no problem of "dirty hands". Good men and women can either avoid war altogether and pay the penalty that the state exacts, or they can participate with a clear conscience, with regrets probably, with doubts even, but not with a justified sense of guilt.

Basil the Great, however, takes a more serious view, a position midway between Tertullian's outright rejection and Augustine's compromise. Regret becomes uncleanness or impurity which, although it may be distinguished from justified guilt, is closely allied to it and may indicate the origin of the "dirty hands" concept.

> Homicide in war is not reckoned by our fathers as homicide; I presume from their wish to make concession to men fighting on behalf of chastity and true religion. Perhaps, however, it is well to counsel that those whose hands are not clean only abstain from communion for three years. (*Letter*, CLXXXVIII, 13)

MACHIAVELLI: COMPROMISE AND EXPEDIENCY

Machiavelli (1965) presented a deliberate approach to compromise and expediency. The Prince must learn how not to be good if he will survive:

> There is such a difference between how men live and how they ought to live that he who abandons what is done for what ought to be done learns his destruction rather than his preservation, because any man who under all conditions insists on making it his business to be good will surely be destroyed among so many who are not good. Hence a prince, in order to hold his position, must acquire the power to be not good, and understand when to use it and when not to use it, in accord with necessity. (*The Prince*, Chapter XV)

Machiavelli was not making a case for placing politics in an autonomous realm, beyond the claims of ordinary morality. He was judging the good prince, "among so many who are not good" by the same code which he himself respected. Elsewhere he approved of the Florentines who have a higher regard for their "*patria* than for their souls". In both cases, it is a question of the prior claim of high office; his point is that there are situations in which the good leader must override his personal intuitions about moral obligations in the interests of the state for which he has accepted responsibility.

Similarly, Walzer (1973) is clear that we are dealing with a problem within the moral code, a question of the grounds and limits of compromise. For him, the moral politician is a tragic hero. He (sic) does not shrug off the dilemma as if it were of no consequence, for he is a man of scruple (which is probably why we voted for him). But neither can he adopt the absolutist line and stay pure, for either he would have failed to obtain power in the first place, or he would have lost it in the struggle with "so many who are not good". If he couldn't stand the heat he should have stayed out of the kitchen. What he has is a genuine dilemma, the problem of "Dirty Hands".

> If he is the good man I am imagining him to be, he will feel guilty, that is, he will believe himself to be guilty. That is what it means to have dirty hands

… Here is the moral politician: it is by his dirty hands that we know him. If he were a moral man and nothing else, his hands would not be dirty; if he were a politician and nothing else, he would pretend that they were clean. (p. 166ff)

SARTRE: "DIRTY HANDS"

The starkest presentation of the case for compromise and expediency is to be found in Sartre's *Les Mains Sales* (1955). In it, Hugo, an idealist, intellectual revolutionary (an absolutist) believes he ought to assassinate the leader of his party, Hoederer, for betraying the revolutionary principles for reasons of opportunism. Hoederer's reply has become much quoted:

> How you cling to your purity, young man! How afraid you are to soil your hands! All right, stay pure! What good will it do? Why did you join us? Purity is an idea for a yogi or a monk. You intellectuals and bourgeois anarchists use it as a pretext for doing nothing. To do nothing, to remain motionless, arms at your sides, wearing kid gloves. Well, I have dirty hands. Right up to the elbows. I've plunged them in filth and blood. But what do you hope? Do you think you can govern innocently? (p. 224)

Here we find neither the absolutist, rejection of compromise, as desired by the unworldly Hugo, nor the uncomplicated, clear conscience adoption of the "filth and blood", as might be argued by the act utilitarian. Keeping one's hands clean is not an option in Hoederer's eyes. His position is that of the leader who knows only too well that it is not possible to "govern innocently". His political dilemma is a real one.

THE DILEMMA OF NUCLEAR DETERRENCE

In recent years, van Gelder (1989) has drawn attention to two "dilemmas of deterrence", the credibility dilemma and the usability dilemma. Although van Gelder saw these as two closely related questions, they can be better described as one, a dilemma with two horns: loss of credibility and likelihood of use. Briefly, the more extreme our threats to use nuclear retaliation, and therefore the more likely to lead to all out nuclear war, the less credible it will be that rational people would carry them out, and deterrence fails. If, however, we moderate the threats in order to make them more credible, they may then become insufficient to counter the possibility of aggression.

> Nuclear deterrence cannot be effective unless its threats are credible, and yet the very process of making those threats credible increases the risk of nuclear war, directly undermining the original purpose. Nuclear deterrence appears to be either incredible or self-defeating; either way, it fails to prevent nuclear conflict. (p. 159)

This has led to a debate (see, for example, Schonsheck, 1991) in which different escapes from the horns of the dilemma are argued. It would be difficult to decide whether this is a moral or a non-moral dilemma. What is clear, however, is that it illustrates typically the different principles that come into play when defining a credible defence policy for a country and the impossibility of keeping one's hands pure.

WIDER APPLICATIONS

There are many other applications of this problem. Benn (1983) described the issues from the point of view of the liberal conscience, as the conflict between the 'personal' and the 'political'; in this the liberal has a conflict between two principles which he acknowledges. On the one hand, the obligation to be tolerant, a tradition born out of the wars of religion and persecutions of the sixteenth and seventeenth centuries, which has taught him advantages of respecting the individual conscience, the "Inner Light" and the right to individual belief. The integrity of the individual demands such respect; it is also a prudent policy, for the sake of social peace. It was on these grounds that the U.K. Report of the committee on Homosexual Offences and Prostitution (*The Wolfenden Report*) declared in 1957 that "there must remain a realm of private morality and immorality which is, in brief and crude terms, not the law's business" (Cmd. 247, para. 61).

On the other hand, liberals understand morality to be a rational process, open to public scrutiny and justified by appeal to the commonly accepted criteria of good reasoning. They therefore have difficulty in accepting "gut feelings" or private intuitions. Morality is not a question of personal taste, like baroque music or avocado pears, it is public in the sense that Wittgenstein claimed a language must be public: "the principles, the reasons for saying that you have got it right or wrong, must be open to anyone" (Benn, 1983, p. 156). On similar grounds to these, Lord Devlin rejected the distinctions made in the *Wolfenden Report*: "I do not think one can talk sensibly of a public and private morality" (1965, p. 16).

The question for the liberal, argued Benn, is whether to congratulate one's leaders for making tough decisions in the jungle world of power politics, or to expect some signs of appreciation of the tension between a morality of principles and one of utilitarian expediency. His own conclusion seems to support the "dirty hands" concept and the belief that political dilemmas genuinely exist. In answer to Hoederer' question, he does not believe that it is possible to govern innocently and that "a feeling of loss, for some liberals, is inescapable" (p. 159).

IS THERE A DISTINCTIVE PUBLIC MORALITY?

Let us now look a little closer at the claim that the public sphere is so special that a different morality applies to it. Several reasons can be put forward to justify the distinction between a public and a private morality. First, there is the popular view that politicians are different from (and worse than) private citizens.

Walzer (1973) has drawn a distinction on three grounds between politicians and "other entrepreneurs in an open society, who hustle, lie, intrigue, wear masks, smile and are villains" (p. 162). The first reason which causes them to be regarded as worse than ourselves, he claimed, is because the politician acts on our behalf, he (sic) "hustles, lies, and intrigues for us – or so he claims". As it happens, he cannot serve us without also serving himself, for success brings him the power and glory that he so desires, "the greatest rewards that men can win from their fellows". But he will argue that if he did not hustle and lie there would be many others prepared to do so.

Secondly, a politician is considered worse than the rest of us, he claimed, because he exercises power over us. "The successful politician becomes the visible architect of our restraint. He taxes us, licenses us, forbids and permits us, directs us to this or that distant goal – all for our greater good (p. 165).

Thirdly, the politician uses his power against us. "The men who act for us and in our name are often killers, or seem to become killers too quickly and too easily" (p164). For these reasons, therefore, politicians are arguably distinct from ordinary citizens and are commonly regarded as such. In which case they can be expected to follow a different code of behaviour.

In Public You Are No Longer "Your Own Man"

More generally, with regard to other posts of responsibility, it can be argued that it is no longer the individual's moral code that is relevant. Each one is in office by virtue of election, appointment or nomination and, as such, personal morality is not particularly important; what counts are the multifarious codes of the constituency or the moral standards of the appointing authority. You should therefore seek a consensus, a mandate or delegated duty. However much you wish to be "your own man", you are not. You are under authority and, even though this involves ducking and diving, wheeling and dealing, making the best of the situation, this is what you are put there to do and to imagine otherwise is a selfish indulgence.

By the same token, the moral intuitions appropriate to individuals in their private capacity may be quite inappropriate in their public role. Benn quotes with approval Cecil's observation that "No one has a right to be unselfish with other people's interests" and that the morality, which requires an individual to sacrifice his or her interests to others, is inappropriate to the action of a state (p. 162).

Lying to Save One's Own Skin

When one considers the apparent public outrage in the USA at the lies told during the Watergate affair, or those that forced the resignations in this country over the Spycatcher issue, it is clear that lying to save one's own skin in government is regarded as a very different matter to the grand fabrications of state. As Benn stated it:

> The grim necessities of the contest for power will excuse a lie for the country's sake. To lie for the government's survival can be acceptable, if embarrassing, to its supporters. To lie for personal advantage alone is not acceptable and not

to be excused merely by an appeal to the Hobbesian rules of the political game.
(p. 166)

Then there is the "buck stops here" argument. All those in positions of authority are to some extent isolated. However hard they consult, seek advice, attempt to find the will of the people, this will elude them. They are often expected to take the very decision that no one else will take; it may be to sack a troublemaker, to take a stand against an aggressor or to threaten those who use violence. At the point of decision, it is quite likely that their followers or advisers will look to their own reputations and speak with a forked tongue. They may be criticised and opposed right up to the point of decision; then, if it appears successful, they can expect to be told that this was what they were expected to do all along; if unsuccessful, they will be expected to take the blame, even resign. Such things go with the job.

Power Seduces

Another distinguishing aspect is the seduction of power. Those who obtain high office will not readily relinquish it; politicians can do no good unless they obtain power themselves, and this is unlikely unless they use the necessary means, including making compromises, wheeling and dealing. The struggle to get re elected, or re-appointed may require many such accommodations, face saving formulae, U-turns and the like. Popular acclaim is fickle and to strive overmuch for the appearance of consistency will be regarded by the public as a conceit of far less importance, in most cases, than to undertake dubious backstage manoeuvres in order to retain power.

Yet another approach is to distinguish between the different forms of reasoning that are employed in political and private spheres respectively. Lucas (1966), for instance, argued that political reasoning is dialectical, it balances opposing interests; the questions are never prejudged and the issues rarely settled or closed. This means that both sides in a dispute can always return to them, perhaps years afterwards, when new circumstances apply, when there are new actors on the stage, and new constraints to limit our choices. Oakeshott (1965) expressed the matter slightly differently; when we come to a political argument, he wrote, we bring a whole array of beliefs, traditions, feelings and prejudices. This means there is no body of norms and principles, which can provide tidy solutions or references to guide our decisions. We can, of course, call on our beliefs and traditions, but not in the sense of a vade mecum of ready principles. We learn from these only by living them out in practice and in what are, by definition, new situations. Our decisions are based upon what is likely to provide the most acceptable compromise between competing goals.

Politics Is a Jungle

Many would argue that the distinction between a public and a private morality rests on the fact that politics is a jungle world, where the devil takes the hindmost and the refinements of moral principle are a luxury by comparison with the survival of the fittest. Thus, Benn argued that those who are the agents of the state "are licensed to set aside moral principles for the sake of good outcomes (or more usually, to avoid bad ones), and that the reason for this is that they are the champions and trustees of the public in a jungle world" (p. 167).

There is, therefore, a case for seeing a difference in the role, and a difference in the perception by the public of that role. But it is very doubtful if any of these arguments establish the case that politics (or the military life, or management) is beyond the reach of moral considerations. Accountability makes for greater complexity in ethical issues, less predictability and raises other constraints. All these are arguments for compromise and adaptation of the code, but not for the autonomy of public morality; still less are they for taking politics and other spheres of responsibility out of the moral realm altogether.

Morality applies to all human actions; the distinctions, therefore, if they indeed exist, are within morality. It is clear that a more complex set of considerations applies to posts of public responsibility. There will be a need to obtain publicly desired goals by the best means possible, including compromises. In such circumstances, men will argue about the difference between fighting dirty and fighting clean, between acceptable dealing and unscrupulous actions, between motives of self-interest or personal advantage and the public interest. The politician will not be respected for feathering his own nest, taking back handers or saving his own skin at the expense of the common weal. But in the end Niebuhr's words seem the most applicable:

> Politics will, to the end of history, be an area where conscience and power meet, where the ethical and coercive factors of human life will interpenetrate and work out their tentative and uneasy compromises. (1963, p. 4)

Having considered whether the world of politics, or posts of public responsibility, are protected by a special code of morals and found that the argument is not persuasive, we should look at that underlying view of society which we could call democratic. How do schools prepare students for this?

CONFLICT, COMMON SENSE AND
THE THINKING SOCIETY

The Perspective from Social Psychology

Key Points

- Conflict and contradiction in sociological theory
- The everyday facts of lived practical reason
- Historical inevitability and dialectic
- Dilemma and rhetoric

The claim in this chapter is that dilemmas and differences of opinions are the lifeblood of a thinking society and some of the essential prerequisites of democracy. Students, therefore, should be encouraged to welcome conflicting ideas and examples of contradiction and debate; they should not seek to eliminate disagreement on the mistaken ground of striving for rational clarity; it is not too much to say that, were they to succeed, they would be sowing the seeds of the censorship of unwelcome ideas and providing a breeding ground for fundamentalism. Down this road lie autocracy and ultimately a totalitarian nightmare. The recommendation is that one of the best ways for schools and colleges to avoid these early signs of extremism is to welcome the process of argumentation, the internal disagreements which exist within every person, as marks of common sense and one of the safeguards of our democratic values.

First, however, in order to establish the case for this, it will be useful to consider the perspective from social psychology and to see what light can be shed on the experience of dilemma by anchoring it in its social and ideological context. There will be a survey of some of the main approaches of sociologists and social psychologists towards dilemma and ideological conflict. It will be suggested that most of these theories inadequately explain the existence of real dilemmas in practical living in that they tend to undervalue either the place of history or the thinking and argumentation of individuals. Rather than presenting dilemma as a genuine struggle for the individual or as playing a substantive and necessary part in the development of an individual's capacity to think or in creating a society in which argumentation flourishes, most theories hitherto apparently seek to explain or avoid it.

The approach recommended here is a "return" to common sense one, as advocated elsewhere (see Chapter 4). It will suggest that dilemmas are not only a natural part of society but also a necessary precondition of the development of common sense, for liberal thought and much we take for granted in Western democracies. Focusing finally on the views of Billig (1988) and the Loughborough Discourse and Rhetoric Group, it will be argued that common sense grows only in a certain soil and that ideological dilemma should be regarded as essential for developing the ability to argue, to make comparisons and for the very existence of a thinking society.

CONFLICT AND CONTRADICTION IN SOCIOLOGICAL THEORY

If we are seeking a justification of dilemma as a genuine struggle for the individual to choose between at least two valid alternatives, it will not be easy to find it in sociological theory. On the face of it, sociological analysis, under the influence of Hegelo-Marxist ontology, has much to say about contradiction and conflict in society. In the main, however, these concepts mean an opposition between classes, world views and social forces; for Marx, at least, the means by which contradiction was eliminated was revolution. Sociological theory has especially recognized the place for ideological conflict. But the tendency has been to present this as between ideologies rather than to find a place for dilemma within them.

It seems that sociologists are not especially concerned with the meaning or rational consistency of dilemma, rather they focus upon the circumstances and preconditions of its occurrence in society. They are not particularly interested in the agonies of choice, the decision-making process, the moral development of the individual or the extent of a person's predisposition to recognize valid alternatives. Sociologists in general, and social psychologists in particular are more concerned to devise theories which explain the existence of conflict and contradiction within society, between ideologies, cultures and interest groups on the one hand, or within individuals on the other.

Contradiction Means "Anything Goes"

There are many ways in which the existence of genuine dilemmas can be explained away. One is to use (or rather, as is claimed here, to misuse) scientific reasoning. This chimes with the rationalist stance considered earlier (chapter 2) and the demand for logical clarity. Ryle (1953) considered that "dilemmas derive from wrongly imprinted parities of reasoning" (p. 67) and Flew (1975) wrote:

> If contradiction is tolerated, then, in a very literal sense, anything goes. This situation must itself be totally intolerable to anyone who has any concern at all to know what is in fact true. (p. 17)

It is possible in this way to study dilemma as a disembodied concept with its own rationality (or lack of it), disregarding the human involvement, the perplexities and distress surrounding the process of decision making. By saying "it is time to bring in reason", Hare (1981, p. 31) demonstrated that to display a concern for human perplexity is an intrusion which clouds the main issue, which is whether or not dilemmas can properly be said to exist at all.

The Everyday Facts of Lived Practical Reason

This standpoint, however, fails to distinguish between logical confusion and a conflict of values. It also overlooks the fact that science itself is not immune to controversy both in its theory and its method. By contrast, the phenomenological approach welcomes attention to the details of dilemmatic situations; it compels us to anchor the study of personal dilemma, whether this is the concept or the process, in the empirical experience itself. Disembodied ethical theories have no place in this approach. As Macintyre (1985) has said:

> We have to learn from history and anthropology of the variety of moral practices, beliefs and conceptual schemes. The notion that the moral philosopher can study the concepts of morality merely by reflecting, Oxford armchair style, on what he or she and those around him or her say and do is barren. (p. ix)

If we observe closely the experience itself (being faithful to the data, listening to the evidence) we are led inevitably to a respect for what Nussbaum (1985) called "the every day facts of lived practical reason" (p. 5). It seems truer to the spirit of scientific discovery to ground one's reasoning upon the observed evidence, even if this involves the inconvenience and untidiness of a humanistic study.

Historical Inevitability and Dialectic

Other sociological theories can also destroy the substance of dilemma. At first sight, dialectical philosophy finds a positive place for contradiction within the historical process. Hegel (1975a) wrote: "Life involves the germ of death, and ... the infinite, being radically self contradictory, involves its own self-suppression" (p. 117). If, however, his views on the role of tragedy in finding a resolution of conflict are representative of his thought on social conflict, Hegel (1975b) believed that "eternal justice is exercised on individuals and their aims in the sense that it restores the substance and unity of ethical life with the downfall of the individual who has disturbed its peace":

> The truly substantial thing which has to be actualized, however, is not the battle between particular aims or characters, although this too has its essential ground in the nature of the real world and human action, but the reconciliation in which the specific individuals and their aims work together harmoniously without opposition and without infringing on one another. (p. 1197)

In the same way, Engels (1957) developed a theory of historical inevitability and his arguments that thesis is followed by antithesis and then synthesis similarly devalued any belief in genuine dilemma. Contradiction is seen as part of life's mystery but does not describe real disagreement between individuals; dialectical conflict is part of the inevitable flux of history, the pattern determining social change, just as it determines individual values.

Marxist theory, inheriting a philosophy of dialectic, taught that a person's consciousness was determined by his or her social, especially economic, being. There is as a result a genuine place for ideological conflict between economic groups or classes, and the concept of revolution was intended in part as a theory of conflict elimination. Althusser (1979) developed the Marxist concept of ideology and proposed that socialism might reveal as strong a tendency towards contradiction as modern capitalism. In the main, however, this tradition is more intent upon the removal of conflict than on tolerating it. In any case, ideology was seen as a coherent, internally consistent social structure, within the broader whole and this fails to give due weight to the contradictory nature within each ideology or culture.

Living in a Permanent Dilemma

Non-Marxists are also often reluctant to accept the existence of dilemma. For Weber, perhaps the closest parallel is to be found in his idea of "disenchantment" in *Science as a Vocation* (1970), the sense of loss in the face of modernity, in which not even death has a meaning. Such is the traumatic influence upon the individual of the profit motive and the materialistic ethic underlying modern capitalism that the resulting disorientation has much in common with the notion of living in a permanent dilemma. There is such a strong sense of nostalgia for good things now ruined that one can only call it despair. The resulting attitude can be seen in his essay on *Politics as a Vocation* (1970), in which he reveals his reaction to a pietistic upbringing, yet reluctance to accept a Marxist interpretation of the world:

> The devil is old; grow old to understand him! ... Age is not decisive, what is decisive is the trained relentlessness in viewing the realities of life, and the ability to face such realities and to measure up to them inwardly. (p. 125)

On the other hand, feminist writers (e.g., Adams & Cowie, 1990), although too heterogeneous a group to classify with any confidence, seem to reveal an acceptance of, and even a respect for, the idea of dilemma in society. Perhaps it is most clearly articulated in their descriptions of the distance and opposition between theory and political action.

Ideologies and Utopias

Mannheim (1991) wrote that he was "concerned with how men [sic] actually think" (p. 1) and to understand this one must take into account the social implications. For him, ideologies are figments of the mind which disguise the true nature of any given society. They arise unconsciously. Utopias on the other hand are "wishdreams" that inspire opposing groups to act collectively with the aim of revolutionising an entire society. "A state of mind is utopian when it is incongruous with the state of mentality within which it occurs" (p. 173), and in this way conflicts can emerge between utopian beliefs.

> The world is known through many different orientations because there are many simultaneous and mutually contradictory trends of thought (by no means of equal value) struggling against one another with their different interpretations of "common" experience. (p. 241)

Throughout this work, an important aim for Mannheim was to have a view of the whole, which, he claimed, was not possible in modern philosophy or in empirical science. To him, ideologies were whole constructs and utopias were subtypes. The weakness of this ideal-type approach to resolving dilemmas is seen when applied to individual cases. Mannheim's analysis of the debate between Marx and the anarchist Bakunin (p. 219f) reveals that his interest was not in the argument itself, but rather in the way the dominant ideology eventually eliminated the utopian subtype. The conflict thus was resolved without the need to pay attention to the personal dilemma. Indeed, as he put it, the individual case is of less significance than the whole process: "No single individual represents a pure embodiment of any one of the historical-social types" (p. 189). It can be seen that Mannheim had an appreciation of the social and historical influences on the way we think but underplayed the place of dilemma in individual patterns of thought or in the development of common sense.

Berger and Luckmann (1971) likewise took as their starting point the root proposition which they based on Marx, namely that man's consciousness is determined by his social being (p. 16). They therefore demonstrated a concern for social processes, which they distinguished sharply from the philosopher's concern for truth and validity. They were interested in whatever "passes for moral". This permitted them to accept the relativism which is the precondition of much cultural dilemma. They quoted with approval Pascal's maxim that what is truth one side of the Pyrenees is error on the other ("*Vérité au deçà des Pyrénées, erreur au delà*", *Pensees* v. 294).

Their aim was to explain the ways in which symbolic systems in modern societies are socially constructed and to offer an explanation of how contradictions are either eliminated or ironed out. This they did by considering four types of "machineries": mythology, theology, philosophy and science. The first two contained inconsistencies, which were explained on the grounds of their simplicity. Neither myth nor theology (only slightly less naive), contained conflicts which could be considered substantial. Philosophy and science remove dilemma by means of two more mechanisms, therapy and nihilation. Successful therapy:

> Establishes a symmetry between the conceptual machinery and its subjective appropriation in the individual's consciousness; it re-socializes the deviant into the objective reality of the symbolic universe of the society ... Nihilation, in its turn, uses a similar machinery to liquidate conceptually everything outside the same universe. (op. cit., p. 132)

In each case, dominant perspectives are secured by the rejection of alternatives and the dilemma is effectively removed.

The Individual and Inner Forces of Conflict

By contrast, other theories place too great an emphasis upon the individual in society. If we can extend the concept of dilemma to include that of "double purpose", Freud (1901) found a central place for it in his analysis of the unconscious sources of motivation; psychotherapy has as one of its tasks in his tradition, the accommodation of each individual to the inner forces of conflict. Little attention is paid here to the part played by society; dilemma, would therefore seem to be accepted as a normal part of one's psyche, not automatically eliminated.

In Chapter 6 it is shown that Festinger considered the main motivation of each person is to achieve balance and harmony. If there is any inconsistency, therefore, between the choice and the afterthought, the person will find this too uncomfortable and be led to seek a reconciliation. The dilemma remainder therefore disappears. It is as if, as Billig (1988) put it:

> There is for each individual a blood red silicon chip which organizes thoughts and actions. This chip is the psychologist's Rosetta Stone: if only it could be discovered and then decoded, the hidden plan of the mind would be revealed. (p. 19)

This approach also effectively denies the substantive existence of dilemma for the individual because he or she is internally motivated to see that it disappears and harmony returns.

Other individualist interpretations stress the cognitive processes and the way decisions are taken (e.g. Hamilton, 1981). Each individual requires rules and procedures in order to process the incoming data. This is essential in order to select the information, direct thought and action. Dilemmas are explained as mere occasions in this process of organizing information. Data would be selected in order to confirm prejudices. Racists, right wing and left wing theorists would all discover evidence to support their views. Such schematic processing will tend to avoid any inconsistency, double standards or clash of values. In this way cognitive social psychologists also evade the reality of dilemma for an individual.

Explanations of dilemma which stress only the individual, isolated from his situation and background, do not square with the insights of classical tragedy. As Nussbaum (1986) argued, Greek tragedians appreciated that we are not untouched by our environment; fate plays a hand. Conditioning, in modern parlance, is a central factor for us all. We therefore need to appreciate not only the inner struggle of dilemma as a substantive, real event but also at the same time see each person as sharing in the "common sense" of society. We grow in the soil of our environment and upbringing:

I am an agent but also a plant and much that I did not make goes towards making me whatever I shall be praised or blamed for being; that I must constantly choose between competing and apparently incommensurable goods and that circumstances may force me to a position in which I cannot help being false to something or doing some wrong; that an event that simply happens to me may, without my consent, alter my life; that it is equally problematic to entrust one's good to friends, lovers or country and to try to have a good life without them – all these I take to be not just the material of tragedy but everyday facts of lived practical reason. (Nussbaum, 1986, p. 5)

DILEMMA AND RHETORIC

Billig (1988) studied dilemma from the point of view of a social psychologist (he and his co-authors formed the Loughborough Discourse and Rhetoric Group). They criticised both those writers who undervalue the place of history and the influence of ideology in our culture and those who ignore the importance of the individual making concrete and real choices. The authors' definition of dilemma is close to that adopted in this research. Dilemmas are a real and tough choice between two alternatives; as such they are a natural and common part of our lives. But they went much further than this:

What is involved is clearly not a straightforward issue of choice, of alternative courses of action, nor on the other hand a matter of intellectual puzzles or paradoxes. The characteristic of a dilemma which makes it significant for social analysis is that it is more complex than a simple choice or even a straightforward technical problem … (dilemmas are) social situations in which people are pushed and pulled in opposing directions … They are also seen to impose an assessment of conflicting values. (p. 163)

Dilemmas, it is claimed, are built into our culture and contradictory elements can be found within both ideology and common sense. They are necessary for us to develop as thinking human beings. The authors, therefore, intend:

To oppose the implications of both cognitive and ideological theory, which ignore the social nature of thinking. In contrast to the cognitive psychologists, we stress the ideological nature of thought; in contrast to theorists of ideology, we stress the thoughtful nature of ideology. (p. 8)

They distinguished between a lived ideology, "which refers to ideology as a society's way of life", and an intellectual ideology, "which is a system of political, religious or philosophical thinking and, as such, is very much the product of intellectuals or professional thinkers" (p. 27). They believed that:

The study of dilemmas should not be confined to actual choice-making behaviour. There is a need to recognize the dilemmatic aspects of thought, which are preconditions for any dilemmatic choice and which continue to exist in common sense, even in the absence of actual situations which necessitate the taking of difficult choices. (p. 24)

Their argument was founded upon four main points: first, "thinking is necessary for a society and … a society without thought is either an impossibility or a totalitarian nightmare" (p. 149).

Conflict and Dilemma – Essential Prerequisites of a Thinking Person

They believed that dilemmas will always be with us and that they fulfil a vital function. We should not dream of "a silent society, in which all dilemmas have been resolved and whose members, in consequence, have nothing to deliberate about" (p. 149). This, however, does not mean that the issues will be the same in every society, let alone that every society should think in the same way as do people in twenty first century Britain.

In their view, most social psychologists, when they study dilemmas, have seen them in terms of making difficult decisions. This "prevented (them) from appreciating the dilemmatic quality of much everyday thinking, which can be revealed whether or not individuals are actually faced with decisions to be made" (p. 9). By contrast their concern was to examine the social preconditions for dilemmas, in order to show how ordinary life is shaped by dilemmatic qualities. Ordinary people who may not experience the Scylla and Charybdis of dramatic choice, nevertheless are well aware of those conflicting points of view "which surface so vividly in the dilemmatic situation per se " (p. 9).

Second, they believed that thinking, arguing and ideology were closely interdependent. Billig (1991) wrote that "the holding of opinions is an essentially rhetorical and argumentative matter. Moreover, it is also deeply ideological" (p. vii). In each individual, thinking takes the form of an "internal dialogue" or debate, a skill akin to the rhetoric which was so prized and developed in Greek and Roman education (for example by Quintilian, Aristotle, Socrates). They held that there was much to be learned from the insights of these classical writers who so influenced European education.

However, the revived interest in rhetoric has a new emphasis. Traditional rhetoric concentrated on the speaker, on training those who wished to be an orator, to communicate. Modern rhetoric shifts the focus to the listener, or reader (for all discourse now falls within the rhetorician's interest). Under the influence of modern philosophy, the duality of knowledge and opinion, persuasion and conviction, reason and emotion is challenged. Phenomenologists and existentialists would claim that a person's basic method of judgment is argumentation, whether in dialogue with others or with a text; the results, in either case, are necessarily relative and temporal. Not only the processes of the speaker's mind are of interest, but also the response of the audience. The elements of speech, metaphor, allegory, antithesis, parallelism, and so forth, are all a crucial means of studying the transactional nature of discourse.

Potter and Wetherell (1987) argued that people were not necessarily consistent in their attitudes, they did not hold a single opinion but rather used complicated and sometimes contradictory ideas and patterns of speaking. It is as if a living dialogue is taking place within each person. It is also crucial to consider the context in which the speaker may be operating. One example of how this may raise dilemmas is described by Edwards and Potter (1992). They particularly highlight what they refer to as the "dilemma of stake":

> The dilemma of presenting factual reports while being treated as having a stake in some specific version of events or some practical outcome. The recipients of such reports may well, in turn, respond to them accordingly, as designed to manage that dilemma. So, by offering a report rather than, say, directly making an accusation, speakers do not ensure a certain interactional outcome, but seek to garner the accountability of 'just telling it how it is'. (p. 7ff)

Billig went further and argued that conflict and dilemma were therefore essential prerequisites of a thinking person:

> By stressing the dilemmatic and rhetorical nature of thinking, we see thinking as inherently social. In fact, thinking is frequently a form of dialogue within the individual (op. cit. p. 6) ... Thus, the paradox of the term "the thinking society" describes the reality that our dilemmas of ideology are social dilemmas and that our ideology cannot but produce dilemmas to think about. (p. 7)

Third, he saw dilemmas as genuine conflicts for the individual. He is sceptical of social theorists and theorists of ideology, who tend to give weight to the processes of history and how they create the culture and beliefs of particular societies but tend also to "ignore the thinking of individuals, for individuals are often seen as the blinded bearers of a received ideological tradition" (p. 2). On the contrary, Billig claimed, whereas people may not have invented the common sense which they use, they are not "dupes" and each individual is a thinking person, not "his master's voice":

> Conflicts are of interest ... not to find how they might be institutionally resolved or functional for the social system, but to show how they give rise to both problems and opportunities for reflection, doubt, thought, invention, argument, counter-argument. Hence our conception suggests that in everyday thought the individual is a lay philosopher, not a marionette dancing to the desires of a great design. (p. 163)

Antithetical Proverbs

Fourth, their interest did not lie in the motivation or information processing of individuals but in the fact that knowledge is socially shared and that common sense includes conflicting and contradictory notions. The authors quoted a number of classical sayings and proverbs to illustrate how normal and natural a part of life dilemma is. In particular, they refer to Francis Bacon who, in his *Of the Dignity and Advancement of Learning* (1605), collected a number of antithetical proverbs (see Whately, 1963, appendix A), which by their seeming contradiction reveal how dilemma is woven into the heart of our practical wisdom. Today, in our upbringing, we are still receiving contrasting messages from our traditional proverbs: "Absence makes the heart grow fonder" on the one hand, and "out of sight, out of mind" on the other; "nothing ventured nothing gained" but "look before you leap"; "many hands make light work" but then "too many cooks spoil the broth"; "charity begins at home" yet "love thy neighbour". Similarly, we have come to accept as normal Hamlet's predicament that it is sometimes necessary "to be cruel, only to be kind" (Act 3, Sc.4).

Billig argued that such dilemmatic contrasts are necessary if we are to learn how to think at all and that fireside wisdom, even though frequently contradictory, assists in the very development of our thinking and arguing processes.

> The contrary themes of common sense represent the materials through which people can argue and think about their lives, for people need to possess contrary themes if they are to think and argue. (p. 8)

He then undertook some "initial investigations", "key illustrations" of real and concrete dilemmas which confront individuals in specific situations: education, medical care, race and gender. The authors identified common ideological themes which recurred in these discourses. They drew out the tensions between authority and equality, freedom and determinism, the individual and the state. The same conflicts occur frequently whatever the dilemma being considered. They concluded:

> In this way the characteristics of dilemmas are revealed as fundamentally born out of a culture which produces more than one possible ideal world, more than one hierarchical arrangement of power, value and interest. In this sense social beings are confronted by and deal with dilemmatic situations as a condition of their humanity. (p. 163)

CONCLUSIONS

This analysis supports the educational aims of this book. In the first place it elaborates the original definition and understanding of dilemma. It accords closely with what Hampshire wrote (1980) and it gives due weight both to the individual and to the constraining influence of his or her cultural environment. As Gaut (1993) pointed out when she argued that "a reflectively improved version of common-sense morality is the best morality":

> We already possess a raft of moral convictions, which has been passed on to us by our parents and fellows from our culture, altered and refined by the common understanding of previous ages, and which we, in turn, will pass on to

our descendants after we have made our own reflective contributions. Ethical convictions and deliberations are always historically located and conditioned. These inherited convictions are those of common-sense morality. (p. 33f)

Secondly, the perspective we have been considering stresses the place of "common sense" and the importance of developing the capacity to debate different sides of a question. It shows the ideological basis to many recurring dilemmas (e.g., between individuality and collectivity, equality and authority, freedom and necessity). It sees dilemma as a constant in society and does not aim to remove it (or discover a method of resolution); it does not look forward to the end of dilemma, "towards a pure consistency of thinking, for that would be to look forward to the end of thought" (p. 148).

In this way the experience of dilemma is left centre stage and of permanent significance in the life and thinking of any individual, indeed of society itself. For these reasons alone, it supports the claim for a more important place in our educational programmes for the consideration of dilemmatic situations.

It is important to prepare students for the world of psychological "explanations" which awaits them; explanations for what they are doing when they wrestle with dilemmas, for the process of decision making and for the concepts surrounding this, such as "post decisional regret", problem solving or guilt. To this we must now turn.

YOUNG ADULTS, DILEMMAS AND DECISION MAKING

The Perspective from Psychology

Key Points

- Stages in moral development
- Adult reasoning, relativism and empathy
- Cognitive dissonance
- Problem solving
- Cognitive abilities and types of thinking

If schools and colleges are to prepare students for a world in which they will be expected to take decisions, some of which will certainly be difficult and marginal, it would be helpful to try and understand the process of decision making and to look at some theories of cognitive development and ideas on the growth of moral awareness which underpin those decisions. To help teachers do this is the purpose behind this chapter.

It also provides an important perspective on dilemma because, unlike the philosophical viewpoint, which is concerned mainly with meaning, and rationale, or the sociological, which looks at the social preconditions, psychology sheds light on the concept by focusing more on the processes of thought, of decision making and of cognitive development; it is more interested in the personal perception of dilemma and the moral awareness that this presupposes, than in the social context or environmental circumstances. It raises the question whether or not there is a case for believing that there is a special type of "dilemma thinking"? These are surely important ideas for students to grasp before entering the workplace.

It is quite common to see the terms "thinking", "problem solving" and "cognition" used interchangeably, based on the definition that "thinking is what happens when a person solves a problem" (Mayer, 1977, p. 6). There are of course many different theoretical approaches to the psychological understanding of "thinking". Two such opposing views are considered: one is to define thinking as an external, behavioural manifestation, subject to empirical observation, the other as an internal, cognitive process. Behaviourists do not find it helpful to consider thinking as an internal process without relating it to visible evidence. Cognitive theorists on the other hand, understand thinking to be an internal mechanism underlying behaviour but separable

© KONINKLIJKE BRILL NV, LEIDEN, 2018 | DOI 9789004368118_007

from it. Gilhooly (1982) used the term to refer to "a set of processes whereby people assemble, use and revise internal symbolic models" (p. 1). Others, like Mayer, adopt a compromise position, in which thinking is a cognitive activity inferred from observable behaviour, but nevertheless an internal process to be studied in terms of the cognitive system, its purpose being directed towards finding solutions or solving problems.

This chapter also shows that the recognition of dilemma (i.e. the acknowledgment of valid alternatives) has much in common with certain aspects of adult reasoning, such as: the acceptance of genuinely conflicting obligations, the tolerance of ambiguity, openness to relativism, the influence of the specific situation and context. These are arguably the characteristics of mature thinking and the later phases in cognitive and ethical development.

FORMAL OPERATIONAL THOUGHT

Piaget represents a vital starting point even if later criticised. His theory of cognitive development involved a clinical, detailed questioning of children in a number of problem situations and from his experiments he produced a descriptive analysis of the development of basic physical, logical, mathematical and moral concepts from birth to adolescence. For him, formal operational thought was the final stage in the sequence of cognitive development and must therefore represent his view of the nature of mature thinking. His theory has been summarised by Child (1986, p. 145) as genetic (the higher processes evolve from biological mechanisms), maturational (in that they formed an invariant sequence through several clearly definable and related stages) and hierarchical (in that each stage must be experienced and passed through in a prescribed order before any subsequent stages of development are possible).

Each stage could be described in terms of the way the individual interacted with the environment (the knower and the known) so that both were mutually transformed. The final stage of formal operations, purported to develop during the years 11 to 16, revealed certain clear characteristics. Formal thinkers are capable of hypothetico-deductive thought, that is to say they can reason like scientists. They construct theories that can be tested by experimentation. Furthermore, formal thinkers are capable of reflecting on their own processes of thought introspectively (thinking about thinking). That is to say they can theorize about mental operations (Inhelder & Piaget, 1958).

STAGES IN MORAL DEVELOPMENT

We have already looked at the place of moral dilemmas in ethical philosophy. The psychologist, however, is concerned with the development of moral judgment and Piaget's study, *The Moral Judgment of the Child* (1932), has been the stimulus for most subsequent research in this field. Kohlberg, a prolific and influential writer (also a pupil of Piaget's) extended this theory and method (1966). He argued that young people progress sequentially through six stages of moral judgment and claimed that adult morality is characterized by the reasoned adoption of absolute principles.

Piaget believed that intellectual development consisted of a sequence of changes in cognitive structures, as a result of both internal and external pressures, and that these structures were set by the structure of the brain. He traced the development from heteronomous reasoning, in which the authority was the adult, to autonomous reasoning, in which the standards and rules were set and determined by the individuals themselves.

Kohlberg similarly believed that moral development occurred through an invariable sequence of stages; he described six steps (compared with Piaget's two basic stages), each with a separate type of moral reasoning, becoming more sophisticated with age. Each stage was quite different but, while Piaget believed moral maturity (autonomous reasoning) was achieved around the age of 12 for most people, Kohlberg's capacity for reasoning in principles might be reached by some (though most would fail to do so) in the late teens. Unlike Piaget, Kohlberg believed that the stages normally spanned the whole of a person's life.

Kohlberg uses one method to establish his theory, the Moral Judgment Scale, a structured test consisting of nine hypothetical dilemmas. The interviewer presents each subject with one of the dilemmas and the person makes a judgment about it and then puts forward a justification for his or her choice. The kind of reasoning used is the basis on which one would know which stage of moral development the person had reached.

Although Kohlberg's theory of moral growth received much acclaim at the time, there were many critics (as there had been for Piaget's theory, and on similar grounds). Kurtines and Greif (1974), for example, pointed out that his research methods were flawed. It was rare, they said, that all nine dilemmas were presented, through shortage of time, so the tests and the scale were neither standardised nor consistently applied. The number and content of the dilemmas varied across the research and as a consequence the results did not allow easily for generalizability. The effect of this was that each study employed a unique scale. "In the absence of evidence demonstrating that each dilemma taps the same cognitive dimension there is no basis for making comparisons among studies using the Moral Judgment Scale" (Kurtines & Greif, 1974, p. 468).

Probably the most long-lasting criticisms will prove to be those against the idea of there being structural "stages" in either moral or cognitive development, which are maturational and hierarchical. Common sense would seem to indicate that individuals operate at various levels at various times and in various domains, and that fixed, age-related stages do not accurately reflect the years of human development.

The importance from the point of view of the study of dilemma is that adult reasoning and moral judgment can be seen as a further development in which the ability to recognize dilemmas emerges. For instance, Kramer (1983) summarised post-formal thinkers as possessing first, an understanding of the relative non-absolute nature of knowledge. Knowledge and reality are viewed as temporarily true (or real) rather than universally fixed. Second, post-formal thinkers accept contradiction as a basic aspect of reality (e.g., an individual might realize that a relationship with another person cannot be described in terms of love or hate alone, but by the simultaneous existence of these apparently contrasting emotions). Third, "post-formal thinkers possess an ability to synthesize contradictory thoughts, emotions, and experiences into more coherent, all-encompassing wholes" (Rybash, 1986, p. 38).

Most writers on adult thinking acknowledge their indebtedness to Perry (1968) who studied the growth of epistemological thought during college years. He was one of the first to consider the place of relativism in mature thinking, describing his research as follows:

> We trace a path from adolescence into adulthood. We map this journey from the accounts of college students … Could it be that in a changing, pluralistic culture in which man's very knowledge and values are seen to be relative, the sequential challenges of this journey are essential steps in a person's maturation? We think so. (p. ix)

Perry described the evolution in students' interpretation of their lives as a progression through various "forms" which characterize the "structures which the students explicitly or implicitly impute to the world" (p. 1). He devised a measure (*A Checklist of Educational Views*), which was administered to a random sample of 313 freshmen in 1954. This was followed up by 98 taped interviews including 17 complete four-year records. The questions were open ended in the form, "Would you like to say what has stood out for you during the year?" Then, "Do any particular instances come to mind?" The development he observed is described in terms of nine positions through which the students are seen to pass. These he summarised as follows:

> Position 1: The student sees the world in polar terms of we-right-good vs. other-wrong-bad. Right answers for everything exist in the Absolute, known to Authority … Position 2: The student perceives diversity of opinion and uncertainty, and accounts for them as unwarranted confusion … Position 3: The student accepts diversity and uncertainty as legitimate but still temporary … Position 4: the Student perceives all knowledge and values (including authority's) as contextual and relativistic … Position 6: The student apprehends the necessity of orienting himself in a relativistic world through some form of personal Commitment… Position 7: The student makes an initial commitment in some area … Position 8: The student experiences the implications of Commitment … Position 9: The student experiences the affirmation of identity among multiple responsibilities and realizes Commitment as an on-going, unfolding activity through which he expresses his life style. (p. 9f)

As far as the study of dilemma is concerned, Positions 1 and 2 clearly represent an inability to "recognize" dilemma whilst the remaining Positions show an evolving accommodation to dilemma in a relativistic world. This interesting study in many ways paved the way for research into adult thinking.

Another study of adolescent moral judgment, supporting the hypothesis of post formal development and relevant to our understanding the ability to perceive dilemma is found in Kitchener and King (1981). They put forward a seven stage model of post adolescent reasoning. High school and college students were administered the Reflective Judgment Interview which consists of a set of four dilemmas in the sphere of current events (science, religion and history) and were assessed according to their understanding of reality and the way they justified their beliefs. The model outlines a sequence of increasingly complex methods whereby they might do this. As they see it, changes occur over age and over educational levels. The most advanced is called "Reflective Judgment". These changes can be seen in the way authority and evidence are used and the increasingly thoughtful examination and evaluation which people give to their experience.

Beyond Formal Operations

Another powerful critique of Piagetian developmental theory, which is directly applicable to the recognition of dilemma, is contained in a collection of essays entitled *Beyond Formal Operations* by Commons, Richards and Armon (1984). This is a symposium of studies on cognitive development beyond Piaget's formal stage. The contributors question the idea that there is a fixed developmental endpoint of cognitive ability, reached in adolescence, a kind of plateau of ability after which there can only be a gradual decline. In contrast, they argue that adult thinking has a sophistication which indicates a further development:

> The model of formal operations is too limited to capture the richness of adolescent and adult thought. Kinds of thinking exist that do not show the logical structure of formal operations or of lower stages. These kinds of thinking might develop parallel to formal operations and supplement them, being used in areas not amenable to the logic of propositions ... There is a great deal of developmental potential beyond formal operations. More sophisticated thinking can be found and described in models collectively labelled "postformal". These models aim at extending conceptions of cognitive development into adulthood. (1984, p. xv)

ADULT REASONING, RELATIVISM AND EMPATHY

Within this symposium, a number of concepts is developed to characterise adult reasoning, of which four are selected here. First, Koplowitz (1984) claimed that there are two post formal stages, a general system stage and a later unitary stage. He illustrated this by comparing two concepts of causality, arguing that the formal-operational concept of causality is a linear one. An event is conceived of as being the result of a previous event:

> The linearity of the formal-operational concept of causality is ... revealed in questions commonly asked about events. "Who started it? "Whose fault is it?"

"How did it begin?" These questions imply a causal chain that has a beginning (p. 273). The general system concept of causality is cyclical. Its difference from the linear formal-operational concept may best be illustrated by means of an example; a formal operational man may feel that he drinks too much and the cause of his drinking is his wife's yelling at him; he may feel her yelling is caused by trouble in the family such as the cutting off of the electricity because the bill was not paid, or the family's being without transportation because he got into an automobile accident ... the wife may feel that she yells at the husband because she is distressed by trouble in the family caused by his drinking ... Both husband and wife have linear concepts of causality and both have an answer to the question, "How does the problem start?" A family therapist, using general system concepts, will not see the problems as having a starting point, but will see the husband's and wife's problems as being mutually causative in a cyclical manner. (p. 278f)

Second, Benack (1984) used Perry's studies (1968) as the basis of an empirical investigation. She agreed with him that the turning point in cognitive growth occurs when students become aware of the existence of a diversity of opinions on any given topic:

Truth externally given is replaced by "truths" each relative to its context of evaluation ... a dualistic world view ceases to exist, except perhaps as a special case of a particular perspective within a relativistic world (p. 341). The dualist sees peoples' experience as generally reflecting the nature of the external world. He or she typically perceives the experience to be identical with reality; not as "how I see things" but as "the way things are". ... With the rise of relativism comes the ability to recognize multiple subjective perspectives on common situations. The relativist is able to differentiate not only "my experience" from "your experience", but "my perspective" from "your perspective". ... He or she sees no contradiction in multiple views of a situation, each having "validity" or "truth". (p. 345)

Benack then applied these ideas to empathy and the ability to be aware of the differences between people without being unduly troubled by them. Benack's hypothesis was that relativistic thought would be associated with higher levels of empathetic functioning. She used a counselling setting to test subjects with a semi-structured interview, inviting them to make concrete moral judgments. Her tests indicated that relativists showed superiority in all dimensions of empathetic functioning.

Third, Sinnott (1984) also described adult thinking as relativistic. "Adults must use relativistic operations to organize their complete understanding of interpersonal and everyday reality adaptively" (p. 300). She considered intelligence to be a question of assimilating reality in order to survive. Two skills are needed: an understanding of interpersonal and social reality and a knowledge of how to apply abstract formal operations selectively. This requires what she called a "necessary subjectivity". Maturity, she argued, brings acceptance of the necessary subjectivity inherent in relativistic operations carried out on reality. This acceptance can be seen in "tolerance of others' beliefs and ways of life". Adolescents and young adults struggle to cope with the inconsistencies in the world by trying to force them into a "correct" formal system. The certainty of formal operations, if they are supplemented by the necessary subjectivity of relativistic operations, can "maximise use of conflicting information and minimize social conflict" (p. 321).

Sinnott acknowledged that relativistic uncertainty is often distressing and individuals may respond with various coping strategies to minimize personal anxiety, probably at the cost of being able to adapt. "A middle aged adult with a family, a career, civic responsibilities, and a social life … is faced with endless demands to "fit" the data of this social world by choosing a viable formal-operational system for interacting with each individual at an appropriate level" (p. 321). Sinnott suggested that, while relativistic operations may not be perfectly consistent with reality, they will provide the best possible match. However, they use mental energy and are stressful. Therefore, individuals resort to various strategies to cope. For example, they can develop a rigid social identity; they can retreat completely and interpret all the behaviours of other people in a simplistic way. Instead of dealing with a certain person as an individual, one may decide to treat that person as a member of a racial group to simplify the choices and judgments that have to be made. On the other hand, "Adults with postformal relativistic operations can act intelligently in complex, everyday situations that require several mutually contradictory systematic logical interpretations" (p. 304).

Fourth, Arlin (1975) is another who supported the theory that there is a further development beyond Piaget's formal operations and she speaks of a fifth stage with two steps: problem solving followed by problem finding. She regarded formal thinkers as primarily involved in the task of problem solving and post formal thinking as primarily geared to the task of problem finding. In 1984 she studied this in a group of young adult artists. All were given several measures of formal thinking and in addition a problem finding task. She found that while all scored equally well in the formal thinking measures, those who were judged as producers of highly creative and original works of art scored significantly better on the measures of problem finding. She also found that less creative artists viewed their work as fixed, unalterable and complete. The more creative artists, however, saw their work as changeable and unfinished.

ADULT COGNITION AND AGEING

Another group of writers, Rybash, Hoyer, and Roodin (1986), considered a number of criticisms of Piaget's theory which, whilst supporting their case for "adult cognition and aging", are directly relevant to the recognition of dilemma.

First, formal operational thought emphasizes the power of logic in problem solving … logical, rational analysis to provide the one correct solution to a

problem, regardless of the domain within which the problem is embedded …
Second, formal operational thinking places an overemphasis on possibility and
abstraction, along with a corresponding under-emphasis on the pragmatics of
everyday life…, the formal reasoner may mistakenly assume that the goal of
mature thought is to construct a set of purified, absolute principles that apply
to problems-in-living. In late adolescence or adulthood, individuals become
aware of this overemphasis on abstraction, absolutism, and logic. (pp. 31–33)

These writers considered that formal thinking was more suited to "closed system"
problems in which a number of finite and knowable variables produce a specific
and reliable outcome. Real life problems on the other hand were "open" in the sense
that there were no clear boundaries between them and the context within which they
occurred. If this is the case, formal thinkers might be expected to approach ethical
and dilemmatic problems in an empirical and rational manner. They would tend to
seek clear solutions and shrink from having to accept conflicting obligations. They
would prefer to solve problems rather than to find them (Arlin, 1984) and would be
ill equipped to understand the relativistic nature of reality and knowledge (Perry,
1968; Sinnott, 1984). All this would cause them to transform unsolvable dilemmas
(or at least those with remainders) into solvable problems.

Rybash et al. (1986) then put forward an Encapsulation Model which analysed
age related changes in cognition. They described cognition as consisting of three
interrelated dimensions, processing, knowing and thinking. These dimensions had
previously been examined in relative isolation from each other by other psychologists
interested in the study of adult cognitive development, and this was an attempt to
draw them together into an integrated theory on adult reasoning.

Our Encapsulation Model integrates and extends the three dominant strands
of adult cognition; processing, knowing, and thinking. Processing refers to the
manner by which various mental abilities and psychological resources are used
to process (i.e. intake) environmental information. Knowing refers to the manner
by which information is represented, stored, accessed and used. Thinking refers
to the manner by which individuals develop an understanding or a perspective
on their knowledge. Specifically, we suggest that information control processes
and fluid mental abilities become increasingly dedicated to and encapsulated
within particular representations of knowledge (i.e. domains) throughout adult
development. As general processes and abilities become encapsulated within
the parameters of domain-ordered knowledge systems, extant knowledge
becomes more differentiated, accessible usable and "expert" in nature. (p. 16)

DECISION MAKING

It is common for writers to distinguish between pre-decisional stress and post-
decisional conflict, or "dissonance" (Festinger, 1957). The questions usually of
most interest to psychologists are, "What types of search, deliberation and selection

procedure do they typically use?" (Janis & Mann, 1977, p. 21) and "How do they make their decision when faced with apparently irreconcilable obligations?"

Decision making has a considerable literature devoted to it from the behavioural sciences but one of the most influential hypotheses was formulated by Simon (1976). Decision makers typically "satisfice" (rather than maximise) themselves, that is to say they look for a course of action that is good enough. People have a limited capability and tend to resort to simplification when dealing with complex decision problems. This applies "whenever the consumer, the president, or anyone else is looking only for a choice that offers some degree of improvement over the present state of affairs" (Janis & Mann, 1977, p. 26).

Sometimes, a modification of this strategy is employed, using a simple moral precept as the sole rule; this is referred to as Quasi-satisficing; alternatively, a multiple rule may be used, Elimination by Aspects, combining several simple decision rules. Then there can be incrementalism, or muddling through. Many people may consider they will be better off moving in small steps towards their chosen goal rather than in "giant strides ... putting out fires, rather than selecting the superior course of action" (Janis & Mann, 1977, p. 33). Etzioni (1967) puts forward a strategy which he calls Mixed Scanning (p. 294), which occupies a halfway position between the perfectionism of optimizing and the casualness of muddling through.

Janis and Mann considered the pre-decisional situation when people are faced with an oncoming disaster (such as a flood, earthquake or crash) and review the symptoms and sources of conflict. Conflict is likely to be intense where a person has to make an important decision at "the risk of suffering serious losses from whatever course of action he selects" (i.e. a dilemma). The most prominent signs will be "hesitation, vacillation, feelings of uncertainty, and signs of acute emotional stress whenever the decision comes within the focus of attention". This leads to such symptoms of stress as "feelings of apprehensiveness, a desire to escape from the distressing choice dilemma, and self-blame for having allowed oneself to get into a predicament where one is forced to choose between unsatisfactory alternatives ("Why did I let myself get into this box? Now I'm damned if I do and damned if I don't", p. 47). The stress is noticeably most acute at the initial stage of decision-making. The example they give is of parachutists' ratings of avoidance feelings, which occur "well before they leave the ground, at the time of their initial decision to participate in the airplane jump ... while on the flight, feelings of avoidance decrease, even though objectively the parachutists are closer to the danger situation" (p. 47). Other avoidance strategies can be used, from simple procrastination to more disguised types of "displacement activity" (see Lorenz, 1966).

Having analysed the causes of pre-decisional stress, Janis and Mann put forward a conflict theory model of stress avoidance. The strategies adopted include: passing the buck ("defensive avoidance"), making snap judgment about the best thing to do ("hypervigilance" or simple panic) and, when there is sufficient time and the individual still hopes to be able to escape unharmed, a high quality decision is possible ("vigilance") typified by the way trained pilots will respond to an emergency. During what they referred to as the "hot cognitive processes" of decision making, there are five stages: (1) Appraising the Challenge (Are the risks serious if I don't change?), (2) Surveying Alternatives (Is this [salient] alternative an acceptable means for dealing with the challenge? Have I sufficiently surveyed the available alternatives?), (3) Weighing Alternatives (Which alternative is best?). (4) Deliberating about Commitment (Shall I implement the best alternative and allow others to know?) and (5) Adhering despite Negative Feedback (Are the risks serious if I don't change? Are the risks serious if I do change?) (p. 172).

Earlier (Chapter 2), it was suggested that dilemmas could be resolved by a reasonable decision but nevertheless leave some kind of remainder in the form of regret for the rejected alternative, remorse or guilt feelings for the outcome. These post-decisional attitudes, painful and undesirable as they are, hold interest for the psychologist. Can they be avoided? One theory which attempts to account for the apparently universal desire to eliminate the conflict between decision and afterthought and to return to a state of harmony is that of "cognitive dissonance".

Cognitive Dissonance

Cognitive Dissonance was first elaborated by Festinger (1957; revised 1964) to describe the situation where two elements, which exist in a person's cognition and which are "relevant to one another but do not for one reason or another fit together". They may be inconsistent or contradictory. Festinger gave the example of a person who is already in debt but nevertheless purchases a new car, or another who is afraid although knowing that only friends were in the vicinity. The presence of dissonance gives rise to pressures to reduce or eliminate the dissonance. "The strength of the pressure to reduce the dissonance is a function of the magnitude of the dissonance" (p. 18). And "It follows from this that the greater the conflict before the decision, the greater the dissonance afterward" (Festinger, 1964, p. 5). Other examples are given of those prepared to continue smoking despite being aware of the consequences, or someone who buys car A despite knowing the superior advantages of car B. According to Brehm and Cohen, who stress the importance of commitment in the theory, the amount of dissonance will depend on the weight given to each element and the degree of commitment to the decision. Brehm and Cohen are concerned with the strategies adopted post decision to reduce the amount of dissonance, to live with the consequences as well as in the applications of the theory to social problems (1962, p. 267f).

By no means all theorists agree with the cognitive dissonance hypothesis and an alternative approach employing a conflict model was proposed by Janis and Mann (1977 and see above p. 85). In this the interest focuses on "hot cognitive processes associated with feelings of regret, which come into play when post decisional conflict is so severe that stage 5 (Adherence) gives way to stage 1 (Challenge)" (p. 309). These symptoms of conflict range from occasional second thoughts to regret, guilt, remorse or anguish; it will be clear that each of these is relevant to dilemma as defined in this study. The essential difference between the conflict theory proposed by Janis and Mann and Festinger's Cognitive Dissonance or Brehm's commitment lies in the importance given to the precise situation in which the decision was taken or the commitment given. The factors which determine whether there is an invariable and spontaneous regret following a decision will be situational, as they explain:

> Our conflict model leads us to expect that the arousal of post-decisional regret and its duration depend upon the conditions under which a decision is made and the conditions that prevail after it is made ... we ... predict that spontaneous regret after a binding commitment will predominantly occur under a rather unusual set of circumstances – namely, when the person believes himself to be fully committed but, because of a premature deadline, continues to vacillate because he is still in a hypervigilant state ... Our model, by rejecting the assumption that post-decisional regret is always present but too subtle or too fleeting to be detected, emphasizes the necessity of searching for situational variables that may determine the intensity and persistence of regret. (p. 335)

Of even greater interest, however, is the nature of guilt.

A Personal Construct Theory of Guilt

The usual definitions of guilt are likely to be either religious or legal; the first is based on the idea that certain actions alienate a person from his or her God, fall short of the requirements of the Church, or fail to come up to the standards and rules of one's religious group (be that a Buddhist monastery, a Catholic order, a Quaker cell or a Moslem group). This distancing from the core of one's belief creates responses we tend to call guilt. These cover misdemeanours or sinful acts. But there is also a more complex idea in Christianity, that of Original Sin, whereby "all have sinned and come short of the glory of God" (Romans 3.23) and are guilty not because of any sins they have specifically committed but simply by virtue of being a member of the human race (see Chapter 3). Legal guilt is more directly derived from the notion of punishment. Actions that are against the law will in many, perhaps in a majority, of cases (given a reasonable government and a law-abiding populace) engender a feeling of guilt.

Kelly (1970), however, sought to develop a "truly psychological definition of guilt" (p. 26). He was critical of religious notions of guilt, basing them (wrongly in my view) on the notion of punishment. For him "even the term 'repentance' which might better be taken to mean rethinking or reconstructing, as its etymology suggests, has come to stand for undertaking something irrelevantly unpleasant or punitive in compensation for disobedience, rather than doing something which will throw light on past mistakes". This, no doubt referring to abuses in the Catholic practice of confession, led Kelly to the conclusion:

> A person who chronically resorts to this kind of penitence to bring his guilt feelings back into comfortable equilibrium, or to write off his wrong-doing,

ends up as a well-balanced sanctimonious psychopath. His only possible virtue is obedience. (p. 27)

He then goes on the draw up a Personal Construct Theory (PCT) definition of guilt "the sense of having lost one's core role structure. A core structure is any one that is maintained as a basic referent of life itself" (except, presumably the sort that Kelly disapproves of as likely to produce "well balanced psychopaths"). A person has only to feel dislodged from such a role to suffer the inner torment most of us know so well.

To feel guilty is to sense that one has lost his grasp on the outlook of his fellow man, or has unwittingly played his part in a manner irrelevant to that outlook by following invalid guidelines … with this goes a feeling of alienation from God, or man, or from both. (p. 27f)

This, apart from his sideswipe at a much abused but nevertheless frequently practised habit of confession, brings Kelly back to the point where his theory can include religious (though less comfortably legal) concepts of guilt. Other writers, especially theologians and sociologists, also recognize the central importance of the sense of guilt in a person's well-being and equilibrium. Here is one example from the PCT tradition:

Guilt can be very damaging to an individual and if the precipitating event is serious enough can become quite debilitating psychologically. For any individual, what is serious may be vastly different, and even an apparently trivial issue to one person may be of such core role import to another as to produce a huge guilt reaction. Where the dislodgment is major the person may end up "consumed by guilt", still hanging on to their original perception of themselves, but unable to deal with the evidence that that is not how they actually behaved. A soldier fit and strong, going into battle, who then avoids a situation in which he might have been killed but has resulted in a mate being killed or injured, might be in such a position. He has always seen himself as one who would rush in regardless of personal safety, but when the crunch came, he discovered he did not with terrible consequences. (Dalton & Dunnett, 1992, p. 59f)

Guilt can sometimes be implanted, perhaps by the persuasive words of an evangelist, or it can be the result of an over-scrupulous conscience, or simply an inappropriate reaction. Nevertheless, no tutor or counsellor, however much they might disagree with a particular instance of guilt faced by a student, should underestimate the debilitating effect of a highly developed sense of guilt. Our churches would be even emptier were it possible for guilt to be removed lightly.

The ability to act, to make decisions between alternatives, to resolve certain types of problem, is clearly wider than cognitive ability. The resolution of dilemma, the motivation to act decisively, opens up the possibility of a skill more akin to creativity; to be able to hold different alternatives in one's mind means being able to empathise with other points of view, to perceive relative truths.

No account of the psychological perspective on dilemma would be complete without looking at problem solving and different types of thinking.

PROBLEM SOLVING

Most definitions of "problem" are derived from the Gestalt psychologist Duncker (1945) for whom a problem arises when a person has a goal but does not know how this goal is to be reached. As Mayer (1977) stated it, there are three characteristics: the given state, the goals or desired terminal state, and the obstacles.

However, such definitions are not particularly helpful in studying the experience of dilemma, being necessarily wide enough to cover problems ranging from geometry to chess and riddles (Mayer, p. 5). What does appear to be agreed by most psychologists is that a task set by an experimenter is not necessarily a problem for a given individual. It may also vanish or be dissolved if the person changes his or her goals (as would dilemma).

Moreover, studies of the influence on each individual of his or her past experience (e.g., of conflicting obligations) appear inconclusive because it may have either a negative or a positive effect. Whilst the "reapplication of very specific, rigid, past habits can hinder productive problem solving, there is of course, complementary evidence that in some cases specific past experience may aid problem solving" (Mayer, 1977, p. 81).

It is important to stress that "dilemma" is not to be confused with "problem". Two main distinctions should be drawn: first there is greater personal involvement in a dilemma than in a problem. This means that whereas the essential element of a problem, as with a puzzle or brainteaser, remains the same, relatively minor changes in a dilemmatic situation (e.g., in age, time, terms of a promise, etc.) could transform the subjective experience itself.

Second, a problem which has been solved does not linger, there is no aftermath (except perhaps pride, relief or exhaustion at completing the task). Dilemmas on the other hand, when they are recalled, even when there are no second thoughts, no remainders of regret or guilt about the rejected alternative(s), conjure up the memory of personal involvement, the commitment, the sense of fear perhaps, or stress, personal tension or urgency.

Despite the insights to be derived from psychological studies of problem solving (or thinking) it must be said that, in general, studies based upon prior learning (often with animal subjects), information processing or the nature of thinking, do not get us very far in our understanding of the recognition of dilemma.

SPECIFIC COGNITIVE ABILITIES AND TYPES OF THINKING

At first it was hoped that perhaps it might be possible to identify dilemma as a discrete form of thinking, a distinctive type of reasoning. Although this proved to be a cul de sac, a potentially fruitful line of enquiry seemed to lie in a comparison between dilemma and different types of thinking, such as lateral, creative, critical thinking and so on.

Following Spearman's use of factor analysis (1904) there have been many attempts to isolate the various components of human abilities. For example, Guilford (1950, 1956) produced a model of the intellect with as many as 120 mental factors, of which he claimed to have identified about 80, including convergent and divergent thinking. The convergent thinker is recognised by an ability to handle problems requiring one correct solution obtainable from the data available. The divergent thinker, on the other hand is capable of addressing problems requiring the generation of several equally acceptable solutions. Guilford attempted to distinguish between the styles of problem solving strategy adopted in closed and open-ended problems, a skill clearly related to that which has been referred to here as recognising dilemma.

Other researchers (e.g., Getzels & Jackson, 1962) have subsequently attempted to confirm the independence of convergent and divergent intellectual operations. They argued, therefore, that intelligence is a broader ability than it was conventionally thought of by those who devised the early IQ tests and that a more systematic map of human abilities might be devised (this point is taken up later in Chapter 10). Yet other work has been done on brainstorming (Parnes, 1977), suggesting that if the mind is allowed to run free in attempting to solve a problem, especially in a group producing as many hypotheses as possible without bothering to evaluate them (think now evaluate later), far more good ideas, and hence possible resolutions, will be generated than by conventional, individual problem-solving techniques. Eysenck, on the other hand, preferred to see creativity as a personality trait and not a cognitive ability at all; as such, he would argue, it is of no relevance to a study of intelligence. A very different approach has been taken by de Bono (1970) who wrote:

> Lateral thinking is closely related to insight, creativity and humour. All four processes have the same basis. But whereas insight, creativity and humour can only be prayed for, lateral thinking is a more deliberate process. It is as definite a way of using the mind as logical thinking – but a very different way. (p. 9)

Lateral thinking is often perverse, preferring the unexpected, illogical; it is provocative "in order to bring about repatterning", it welcomes the chance intrusions (p. 44f). The person who is prepared to acknowledge the validity of alternative viewpoints would very probably demonstrate some of these characteristic ways of thinking as well.

It does not seem as if any agreement has been reached by psychologists on the nature of creative thinking or how to measure it. One problem is the confusing variety of terms used synonymously: "originality", "intuition", "inventiveness", "imagination", "divergent thinking", "creativity", "giftedness" are just some the terms used by psychologists and it is by no means clear how, if at all, they differ in meaning. As Dennis Child (1986) put it:

> The reasons for this difficulty of definition are not hard to find. Consider, for example, the question of aesthetic enterprises in art, music, sculpture or writing. What objective criterion can we use to evaluate the "amount" of

creativity which has taken place in a work of art? Many would rightly say that it is a pointless question anyway because it depends too much upon value judgements within a cultural context. There is no sense in which we can arrive at a widely accepted judgement of creativeness since, in art, music or writing, one man's meat is another man's poison. For this reason, attention tends to have been directed to scientific discovery rather than to artistic creation in the study of creative thinking. There may well be a common thread running through the fabric of our artistic and scientific creativity, but at present we have no idea what it might be ... In the present state of research, the safest conclusion is that divergent thinking is partially dependent on intelligence and partially a function of other personality characteristic. (p. 230)

Alternatively, the study of critical thinking might be thought to be more promising in our search for light on the ability to recognise dilemma. But, again, there are many interpretations of this ability (Bruner, 1964; Feuerstein, 1980; Sternberg, 1985). Three traditions in particular have been concerned to identify what is meant by the term: the philosophical, the educational and the psychological. Sternberg (1986) following the latter defined it as "the mental processes, strategies, and representations people use to solve problems, make decisions, and learn new concepts" (p. 1). This hardly takes us beyond the study of thinking itself.

On the assumption that critical thinking is an analytic skill and therefore at the highest level according to Bloom's taxonomy of educational objectives (1956), many programmes have been planned in the United States to help identify and advance the education of the gifted and talented (see Chapter 3). Sternberg (1986) admitted some of the weaknesses:

We have some good ideas both about how to test it and how to train it. At the same time, we need to recognize some of the limitations on our present understanding. First, we have a much better understanding of analytical (critical) thinking than we do of synthetic creative thinking ... creative thinking seems to be much more resistant to analysis. Yet, the most important contributions of thinking to the world and its cultures are probably in the synthetic domain rather than in the analytic one. (p. 27)

To conclude this digression on cognitive abilities and types and styles of thinking, it should be emphasized that no case is being made here for dilemma thinking being thought of as a distinct *type*. However, many similarities that may emerge between different responses to dilemma, they are covered by the studies on adult thinking already described. There may indeed be similarities but these are insufficient to establish dilemma thinking as a separate category or type of thinking. More important, we would need to allow for those who do not acknowledge the existence of valid alternatives, those who cannot or will not tolerate ambiguity or accept the genuine conflict between obligations. These are, as argued in Chapter 2 above, established standpoints even though I do not share them. Clearly, the student who deliberately rejects the existence of dilemma, or who takes the view that "there is no alternative", would not exemplify the similarities and would provide an exception which would require further theoretical explanation.

It must also be said that the definitions of types of thinking lack the degree of clarity required to make fair comparisons. It is more satisfactory to speak of the Recognition of Dilemma as a style of thinking, as Rybash, Hoyer, and Roodin (1986) concluded about adult reasoning. Having discussed studies that showed that adulthood is characterized by the growth of several components of post-formal reasoning: relativistic thinking, meta-systematic reasoning, problem finding, and dialectic thinking. They stated:

> We concluded that adults think in a manner that is largely consistent with post-formal accounts of cognitive development. However, we have come to the regard post-formal cognitive development as characterized by the emergence of a set of styles of thinking, not as a genuine structural stage of thought. (p. 56)

Clark and Caffarella (1999) employ a four-part typology of adult developmental theories consisting of biological, psychological, sociocultural and integrative models. This enables them to explore within that schema a number of "vexing definitional issues" (p. 4), such as when does someone enter adulthood? Is it, for example in the United States, the age at which a person may work, drive, vote, marry, or join the armed forces, which may differ from state to state but is often taken as eighteen? Or is it the age when a young person begins work and may be responsible for someone else, which might be much younger? Then there are the difficult issues of defining the process of development itself. Also the issues of differences (gender, race and ethnicity, class, education, sexual orientation and so on) and how these issues affect adult development. They make it clear that integration is the preferred model and would seem to be the way forward for future studies. A major point that is being made is that the concept of adulthood has shifted in current studies from seeing it as a condition, or stage, to seeing it as a process or development. Citing Jordan (1978) Clark and Caffarella note, "In our culture, adulthood as a condition used to be simply assumed; as a process it now seems to demand explanation" (p. 3).

The relevance of this for the recognition of dilemma is that when the perspective on adulthood focuses on process rather than condition, it will inevitably emphasise the changes (both internal or psychological, and external or transitional; life events such as birth, marriage and death, or the effects of a disaster, war, flood or tornado. As Taylor (1999) notes, citing Mezirow (1991) "these processes foster thinking that is 'inclusive, discriminating and open to experiences [as well as open] to alternative perspectives ... [rather than thinking that is] rigid and highly defended'" (p. 66). Interestingly, this study offers further evidence that dilemmas can have a positive outcome:

> Change – whether brought about through an intentional transition, 'normative' development, or an unexpected event in life – presents new circumstances

and evidence that cannot be ignored in one's personal meaning system. The resulting conflicts, contradictions, and disorienting dilemmas may stimulate learning. (Rossiter, 1999, p. 83)

CONCLUSION

In conclusion, it has not been argued that the recognition of dilemma is a stage, structure of the mind, faculty or category; dilemma thinking is very probably not a discrete cognitive ability and the evidence so far observed does not support that hypothesis. It is probably more useful to think of RD as a *style*, which is characteristic of maturity, of post formal operational thought (and probably of creative or lateral thinking as well).

As with mature thinking, the boundaries are not clear-cut, and the definition, especially in transition from adolescence to maturity, is necessarily imprecise. We must allow for: (1) An occasional reversion to a previous style of thinking; people are rarely consistent in their level of thinking or "stage" of development across areas of activity. (2) The deliberate choice of an absolutist position or the considered adoption of a "there is no alternative" standpoint. (3) The possibility that some people might deliberately distance themselves from any commitment, preferring to stand aloof from any ethical conclusions. (4) The possibility that some individuals might be retarded or immature in their development and might not reach the later stages of mature reasoning.

CHAPTER 8

LEARNING TO LIVE WITH MARGINAL DECISIONS

The Positive Outcomes of Dilemmas

Key Points

- Recognizing and accepting dilemmas
- The response to "dirty hands"
- Not possible to do good and to save one's soul

RECOGNIZING AND ACCEPTING DILEMMAS

It must now be asked, what insights have been gained that might assist schools and colleges in preparing students to make difficult decisions and live with the consequences? An immediate answer would be to learn by doing, which of course is the reason why there are posts of responsibilities, class representatives, clubs, sports teams, societies, often with a whole framework of debating societies, mock elections, Student Councils, moots and a prefect system.

All this is in addition to the decisions taken daily in the courses, projects and tasks that students sign up to, where the argument has been that dilemmas can be recognised and accepted across the curriculum (Chapter 3).

These are the traditional means of offering students opportunities to participate in democratic structures, to represent others, speak in public and take the consequences of their decisions. These are "the everyday facts of lived practical reason" (Nussbaum, 1986, p. 5). The danger is, however, that on their own they can be no more than an opportunity to practise taking poor decisions, or to react inappropriately (for example, with petulance or violence). To avoid this, what is essential and often missing is an adequate opportunity to reflect on the quality of the decisions. As we have seen:

> The characteristics of dilemmas are revealed as fundamentally born out of a culture which produces more than one possible ideal world, more than one hierarchical arrangement of power, value and interest. (Billig, 1991, p. 163)

It is to be hoped that, given the opportunity to reflect, students could accept that experiencing dilemmas and being able to reflect upon them can be a time of learning and growth. This is partly the meaning behind the observation: "I am an agent but

© KONINKLIJKE BRILL NV, LEIDEN, 2018 | DOI 9789004368118_008

also a plant and much that I did not make goes towards making me whatever I shall be praised or blamed for being" (Nussbaum, op. cit.).

THE RESPONSE TO "DIRTY HANDS"

There is then the question of how students should practise living with their marginal decisions, and how they learn to come to terms with "dirty hands"? What kind of response is desirable from someone whose decisions of office have become tainted by compromise? Attitudes are likely to range from, "I've not given it much thought, since it was the most reasonable thing to do in the circumstances", through, "I regret what I did, but could do no other", to, "I feel very bad about it, and cannot shake off the sense of guilt". These inevitably reflect a variety of ethical standpoints.

Some preliminary points should be made first. For example, it is useful to distinguish those attitudes taken before the action from those adopted after it. The decision itself, together with its consequences, can significantly alter this attitude; it was true of those involved in the Manhattan experiment, developing the nuclear bomb, and it is a well-established phenomenon that those who decide that an abortion is the best solution to an unwanted pregnancy may sometimes subsequently regret it.

Then, it is important to concentrate on the reasons given for a person's decisions, rather than simply on its results. For example, an absolutist, or qualified absolutist like Nagel, will regard some actions as definitively prohibited whatever the situation. Nagel (1971), considering war and massacre, gave as examples the use of flamethrowers or napalm, the bombing of Hiroshima and Nagasaki, and firing on trucks carrying food. Accepting that warfare cannot be romanticised, his hope was nevertheless that "when nations conflict they might rise to the level of limited barbarity that typically characterizes violent conflict between individuals, rather than wallowing in the moral pit where they appear to have settled" (1971, p. 142).

The same outcomes, however, may equally be deplored by a person with a very different ethical outlook. Brandt (1971) argued that the rules adopted by the *U.S. Manual of Warfare* also forbids certain actions (pillage, killing the enemy when they have laid down their arms, or putting prisoners to death because their presence retards his movements). The decision, therefore, where one exists, will be found not in the outcome but in the reasons justifying the decision, the arguments put forward and the motives articulated.

Another pre-decisional characteristic, put forward by Nagel (1971), is that absolutists are more likely to seek ways of retaining direct personal interaction than those relying on expediency of outcome. He suggested that one ought to justify to the victim what is being done to him, a scenario which would sometimes border on the ludicrous:

If one abandons a person in the course of rescuing several others from a fire or a sinking ship, one could say to him " You understand, I have to leave you to save the others". Similarly, if one subjects an unwilling child to a painful surgical procedure, one can say to him, "If you could understand, you would realize that I am doing this to help you". One could even say, as one bayonets an enemy soldier, "It's either you or me". But one cannot really say while torturing a prisoner, "You understand, I have to pull out your fingernails because it is absolutely essential that we have the names of your confederates"; nor can one say to the victims of Hiroshima, "You understand, we have to incinerate you to provide the Japanese government with an incentive to surrender". (1971, p. 137)

This seems pretty far-fetched and more like a case of moral cowardice, a rationalization for doing something in an extreme case that one's absolutist principles actually forbid. If one does decide on torture or blanket bombing, one should of course have an adequate reason for it. The decision may still be wrong, and there may be a real dilemma; but no amount of "direct interpersonal response to the people one deals with" (p. 136) will make it any more acceptable, reduce the amount of guilt, or, one suspects, make it any easier to live with the decision.

The *Articles of the Hague* and *Geneva Conventions* (1899, 1907, 1949) were agreed on all sides; and prior to the subsequent wars it was accepted that aggression should be directed solely at a specific hostile target. But this did not survive the test of one side breaking the agreement. Thus, the allied raids on Hamburg or Dresden were justified at the time as reprisals for German bombing e.g., Coventry and Amsterdam. Civilians, in this respect, will be thought of as impermissible targets.

Alternatively, the law of double effect, whereby indirect results are excusable, has often been quoted. If the undesirable outcome was perceived as an indirect side effect, it was not condemned. This, however, is too vulnerable to the charge of hypocrisy. During the Vietnam War, the American public were not convinced by the argument that their troops were right to raid a village because they suspected that guerrillas were hiding there, nor that they should be excused the killing of hundreds of women and children on the grounds that it was an unfortunate side effect, that killing innocents was not their deliberate goal. There was therefore a public outcry. In this way, popular morality, or common sense, can be a check on the casuistry of government spokesmen.

NOT POSSIBLE TO DO GOOD AND TO SAVE ONE'S SOUL

When we consider what attitudes are appropriate after acquiring "dirty hands", everything depends on the person's attitude to guilt. Clearly, if the utilitarian ethic is espoused, however much there might be a lingering unease or regret, or sympathy for those adversely affected, there will not be any sense of genuine guilt; actions were taken for the best. Similarly, the Machiavellian hero had no serious second thoughts and felt no remorse; he had learned how not to be good and had rejected any idea of personal goodness, in favour of the rewards of power and glory. "A Machiavellian hero has no inwardness", claimed Walzer. We therefore do not know for certain what his feelings were. We can only guess that his attitude is likely to be one of basking in glory.

Walzer found all this very unsatisfactory; "We want a record of his anguish", he wrote. He turned next to the approach taken by Weber in his essay *Politics as a Vocation* (1948). In this, the good man [sic] with dirty hands is still a hero, but a tragic hero, one who does indeed feel the anguish of his decision; one who is no stranger to remorse. But his is a godless career, for the world is an evil place and it is simply not possible both to do good in the world and to save one's soul. The politicians therefore must accept the price of their vocation; by doing bad in order to do good they lose their souls. This seems like an argument to shoot politicians who have dirty hands and then jump into a vat of boiling oil.

How satisfactory is this dualist attitude to the life we lead and individualist account of guilt? We are asked to imagine a man who lies, compromises, sends people to their death, perhaps, but does it all with a heavy, unrelieved heart. He has lost his soul and it cannot be regained. He suffers the inward penalty of individual guilt. But as Walzer says, "We don't want to be ruled by men [sic] who have lost their souls ... a politician with dirty hands needs a soul, and it is best for us all if he has some hope of personal salvation, however that is conceived ... He commits a determinate crime, and he must pay a determinate penalty" (p. 178).

This seems a very unconvincing presentation of the Protestant conscience, if that is what is intended. Some would certainly see the world as an evil place in which the goodness of the Creation has been eradicated by the evil of the Fall. And some might believe that no guilt free dealings are possible within such a world. But most would surely not accept that the "sin" acquired by a secular life cannot be cleansed and was beyond forgiveness? Surely redemption is not foregone by the person who accepts deliberately the political vocation and as such has acquired dirty hands? It is never too late to obtain forgiveness.

INNOCENT CRIMINALS PREPARED TO PAY THE JUST PRICE

Nevertheless, it is the notion of paying a specific penalty that made Walzer prefer the attitude in Camus' *The Just Assassins* (1958). These men are terrorists in nineteenth century Russia; they are heroes who willingly consent to being criminals and to pay the price. There is, therefore, in Camus' eyes no reason to condemn them. They are innocent criminals, "just assassins", because they are willing to die for their actions (p. 215).

Walzer preferred Camus' approach because it indicates a punishment or penance that fits the crime. Sartre's hero Hoederer makes no reference to the moral code by which he has acquired "dirty hands". When he asks the question "Do you think you can govern innocently?" he clearly believes that the answer is "No"; but no further analysis is given. The attitudes of Machiavelli's hero, like his actions, are determined solely by prudential considerations, Weber's tragic and suffering hero is punished only to the extent that as an individual he is capable of suffering. Only

Camus' Just Assassins pay the penalty that society requires. "On the scaffold they wash their hands clean and, unlike the suffering servant, they die happy" (p. 178). This therefore is Walzer's preferred attitude when in the "moral blind alley" which he describes (but see Brandt, 1971, who disagrees).

In the world of public responsibility, we have hard choices to make, based upon our "reflectively improved version of common sense morality" (Gaut, 1993, p. 33). We can either shrug off our moral compromises and decide that in the jungle all is fair, for it is a cold world separated from the human atmosphere of ethical obligations. Or, we can try to purge our guilt in a variety of ways. What is hard to accept is the notion that the world of public affairs brings a different set of moral obligations into play. For example, it is not convincing to argue that, because the business world has profit making and accountability to its shareholders as its main objectives, it is therefore a self-indulgent luxury to find room for private morality. Accountability raises another constraint but does not define a new sphere of activity, and shareholders, like voters, cannot be assumed to be swayed only by amoral considerations.

Whatever moral code is chosen, however, it applies to all human activity, and variations in behaviour, if they exist, are the result of decisions taken within the one moral sphere. The politician will not be respected for closing his eyes to the private ethics of his constituents, on the grounds that they are from a different world. In the end it seems inescapable that reflective common sense in context is our only recourse.

Realizing this, accepting it and learning to live with it, is probably the most positive outcome of experiencing dilemmas, given that a world without them is inconceivable. In such a situation, therefore, schools and colleges can and should be a major influence, not only in recognizing dilemma in all fields of study and human behaviour but also in the development of one's own common-sense morality.

DILEMMAS FROM CLASSICAL LITERATURE

Some Classroom Exercises

Most teachers, sooner or later, will welcome some classroom activities such as subjects for discussion, debate or role-play. The following dilemmas, mostly well known, are drawn from classical literature or contemporary incidents:

a. Ethnic conflicts
b. Getting "dirty hands"
c. Accepting "tainted money"
d. A "sacred duty to yourself"
e. Compromising your sources of information
f. The "murder" of one child to save another
g. Ought the teacher to intervene?
h. Instant reward or "deferred gratification"
i. "Sophie's Choice"
j. Religion and taking up arms
k. Freedom to publish

a) Ethnic Conflicts

You are a female Moslem student whose family tradition is for the women members to wear a veil (Niqab or Yashmak). Some of your friends wear the full Burqa. You are aware that these are not commanded by the Quran but are rather part of the tradition found in the Hadiths and Sunna. However, face coverings have just been banned by your school/college on grounds that they inhibit proper communication, especially with staff, and are a barrier to the full integration of different ethnic groups into the community. Comparisons are drawn to the practice in Holland, Italy, France and some German States where there is a ban of face covering which has been declared legitimate by the European Court of Human Rights. Nevertheless, it is a matter of strong principle to you and your family.

i. *What are you going to do?*
ii. *How do you argue your case?*

© KONINKLIJKE BRILL NV, LEIDEN, 2018 | DOI 9789004368118_009

b) Getting "Dirty Hands"

Your name is Hugo. You are a young, intellectual and very idealistic member of a small revolutionary group that operates within a powerful fascist dictatorship. You discover one day that your leader, Hoederer, has cooperated and compromised with the enemy because, he argues, this will benefit the revolutionary cause in the end.

You, however, are totally opposed to expediency and believe that it is your duty to remain pure and true to your principles. You therefore decide that you must assassinate him. You, the absolutist, go to face him, the compromiser. He turns on you and says:

> How you cling to your purity, young man! How afraid you are to soil your hands! All right, stay pure! What good will it do? You intellectuals and bourgeois anarchists use it as a pretext for doing nothing. To do nothing, to remain motionless, arms at your sides, wearing kid gloves. Well, I have dirty hands. Right up to the elbow. I've plunged them in filth and blood. But what do you hope? Do you think you can govern innocently? (Sartre. *Les Mains Sales*, 1955)

You leave him and reconsider your position.

1. *What are you going to do?*
2. *What are the essential considerations to bear in mind before taking your decision?*

c) Accepting "Tainted Money"

You are the Director of a Charity, which works for the poor and destitute but is itself nearly bankrupt and desperate for funds. The charity is, however, opposed on principle to holding any investments that are known to be in armaments, alcohol or projects likely to harm the environment.

A wealthy and genuine benefactor offers to rescue your charity, but you suspect that his money is "tainted" by profits from these sources. It is your decision whether to accept his offer (Adapted from Bernard Shaw's Major Barbara).

i. *What are you going to do?*
ii. *What are the essential considerations to bear in mind before taking your decision?*

d) A "Sacred Duty to Yourself"

You are Norah (in Ibsen's A Doll's House) faced with the agonising decision whether to leave your husband Helmer, whom you no longer love, in order to return to your parents. Only in this way, you feel, can you develop as a person in your own right and not be a slave to others. It would, however, also mean leaving behind your young children because you have no money while the law would not allow it. Helmer argues that it is your solemn duty to stay with your husband and children:

Helmer:	All your father's want of principle has come out in you. No religion, no morality, no sense of duty ...
Norah:	I must stand quite alone, if I am to understand myself and everything about me
Helmer:	You blind foolish woman! ... It is shocking. This is how you would neglect your most sacred duties"
Norah:	What are they?
Helmer:	Do I need to tell you that? Are they not your duties to your husband and your children?
Norah:	I have other duties just as sacred ... duties to myself. (Act 3)

i. *What are you going to do?*
ii. *What are the essential considerations to bear in mind before taking your decision?*

e) Compromising Your Sources of Information

You are the Prime Minister of Great Britain in time of a long-protracted war. Your intelligence services have broken the enemies' codes and also have well placed informers providing you with a flow of invaluable information. You realize that you must be selective when you use it because in doing so you risk the code being changed, the informers discovered and the information drying up.

For some months you have planned a major invasion with your Chiefs of Staff and are now awaiting favourable information before launching it. One morning the Head of Intelligence informs you that there is good reason to believe that an unexpected bomb attack is shortly going to take place on one of your largest cities. If you warn the city authorities, your informers will be caught, the invasion will fail, the war prolonged and lives will be lost as a consequence. If you do not, the city will be devastated.

i. *What are you going to do?*
ii. *What are the essential considerations to bear in mind before taking your decision?*

f) Does the Teacher Intervene?

You are an experienced, respected history teacher in this country, committed to the traditional liberal values of presenting both sides of an argument, respecting the views of the individual and so on. One year, you find that you have in your A level modern history group an intelligent, articulate student who holds highly racist views. In discussions of such issues as Apartheid in South Africa, the rise of the Third Reich and UK immigration policy, the same scenario always occurs; the racist gets the better of the arguments and has a persuasive and, as you see it, pernicious influence on the group as a whole. On the one hand you are offended at his views and the effect he is having on the group, and on the other you uphold his right to hold unpopular opinions. You are trying to decide whether to intervene and provide counter arguments.

i. *What are you going to do?*
ii. *What are the essential considerations to bear in mind before taking your decision?*

g) Instant Reward or Deferred Gratification?

You are a bright student working for your A levels and predicted high grades. In the past you have been a model pupil and always achieved good results. However, you also enjoy the good life and badly want cash in hand, not only because you like the idea in itself but also for your family, who are very short of money.

Many of your friends (and your boyfriend in particular) have left school and got jobs or set up lucrative enterprises. Your parents and teachers advise you to stay on, get better qualifications and go to university. "You will be happier, more successful and probably better off in the long run", they argue. Your friends say: "why fall for this old stuff, get a life now, who knows what will happen in the future?"

i. *What are you going to do?*
ii. *What are the essential considerations to bear in mind before taking your decision?*

h) The "Murder" of One Child to Save the Other

You are the senior judge of three in an appeal court which is considering whether a surgeon should be legally permitted to separate Siamese twins. The decision is split evenly and you have the decisive vote. The twins share a common aorta and this enables Jodie's heart to pump the blood she oxygenates through Mary's body, as Mary's heart and lungs have no capacity to sustain life. The sad fact is that Mary is incapable of independent existence and she is therefore living on borrowed time, time borrowed from her sister.

It is common ground that Jodie's heart will fail in about three to six months and that Mary's death will inevitably follow hers. It is also not disputed that the twins can be separated without significant risk to Jodie, which will leave Jodie living a more or less normal life (not without serious problems, which her devoted parents will in the main be shouldering). The separation will result in certain death for Mary within minutes of the common aorta being severed. The court is placed on the painfully sharp horns of a dilemma. On the one hand it is in the best interests of Jodie that separation takes place: on the other, it is the best interests of Mary that it does not. The court cannot abdicate responsibility and say it is simply too difficult to decide.

The parents are strict and traditional Roman Catholics who have come from the island of Gozo near Malta, hoping to save their children. They do not consent to the operation. In their view matters should be left to the will of God, no surgery should take place. Their Church agrees, adding that it would set a dangerous precedent if the death of one innocent person were permitted in order to save another. "Mary has done nothing which could justify killing her"

i. *What are you going to do?*
ii. *What are the essential considerations to bear in mind before taking your decision?*

i) "Sophie's Choice"

You are Sophie, a mother struggling to survive with her two children in a Nazi Concentration camp during the 1939–1945 war. Hundreds of inmates are being taken out and killed every day. The commandant comes for your children for they are too young to be useful workers. You are beside yourself with anguish and implore him to let them go. He refuses but eventually offers you the choice: you can give him one and the other will be saved (adapted from Sophie's Choice by Styron, 1980)

i. *What are you going to do?*
ii. *What are the essential considerations to bear in mind before taking your decision?*

j) Religion and Taking up Arms

You are a citizen living in Rome at the end of the Fourth century and have recently decided to be a Christian. The Empire is under attack from all sides by foreign invading hordes. There is a call for all loyal citizens to enrol in the imperial army. On the one hand Christianity, as you see it, teaches loyalty, obedience to the state ("Be subject for the Lord's sake to every human institution [1 Peter 2:13]). On the other it seems to teach pacifism, forgiving one's enemies, turning the other cheek and other such sentiments.

You know that this is a matter of controversial debate. One famous church leader argues "it is absolutely forbidden to repay evil with evil". "How can a Christian go to war, in fact how can he serve even in peace time without a sword, which the Lord has taken away from him?" (Tertullian, On Patience and On Idolatry)

Another takes a different view. Certainly you should feel miserable about fighting or killing, but there is no guilt in it. "It is the wrongdoing of the opposing party which compels the wise man to wage just wars; ... Let everyone then who thinks with pain on all these great evils, so horrible, so ruthless, acknowledge that this is misery and if anyone endures or thinks of them without mental pain, this is a more miserable plight still, for he thinks himself happy because he has lost human feeling" (Augustine, City of God, XIX. 7).

    Also: "Homicide in war is not reckoned by our fathers as homicide" (Basil, Letter 188.13).

i. *What are you going to do?*
ii. *What are the essential considerations to bear in mind before taking your decision?*

k) Freedom to Publish

You are on the editorial Board of a satirical magazine. Your journal has a tradition of challenging establishment views, pushing to the boundaries of accepted humour. The cartoons especially cause offence, but you stoutly defend the right to offend.

You have never, as yet, been convicted under either the Obscene Publications Act, or the Public Order Act, although there have been several libel cases brought successfully against your paper.

You have recently published a cartoon of Jesus Christ which various evangelical and fundamentalist groups have objected to, threatening unspecified action, legal and violent, if you do not retract and apologize. Many, however, on your Board regard this as an attack on freedom of speech, and, indirectly, on democratic values.

i. *What reasoning and arguments will you use at the next Board meeting and to the general public?*
ii. *What are the essential considerations to bear in mind before taking your decision?*

REFERENCES

Adams, P., & Elizabeth, C. (1990). *The woman in question*. London: Verso.

Aeschylus. (1956). *Agamemnon: The Oresteian trilogy* (P. Vellacott, Trans.). Harmondsworth: Penguin.

Althusser, L. (1979). *For Marx*. London: Verso.

Aquinas, T. (1964–1975). *Summa theologiae* (T. Gilby, Ed.). New York, NY: McGraw Hill.

Aristotle. (1953). *The Nichomachean ethics*. (J. A. K. Thompson, Trans.). Harmondsworth: Penguin.

Aristotle. (1962). *The politics* (T. A. Sinclair, Trans.). Harmondsworth: Penguin.

Aristotle. (1975). *Rhetoric* (J. H. Freese, Trans.). London: Heinemann.

Arlin, P. K. (1984). Adolescent and adult thought: A structural interpretation. In M. L. Commons, F. A. Richards, & C. Armon (Eds.), *Beyond formal operations: Late adolescent and adult cognitive development* (pp. 258–271). New York, NY: Praeger.

Augustine. (1872). *The city of god* (Vol. 2, M. Dods, Trans.). Edinburgh: T&T Clark.

Basil. (1895). *Letters and select works: Nicene and post Nicene fathers of the Christian Church* (Vol. 8, B. Jackson, Trans.). Oxford: James Parker.

Beauchamp, T. L., & Childress, J. F. (1989). *Principles of biomedical ethics*. New York, NY: Oxford University Press.

Benack, S. (1984). Postformal epistemologies and the growth of empathy. In M. L. Commons, F. A. Richards, & C. Armon (Eds.), *Beyond formal operations: Late adolescent and adult cognitive development* (pp. 340–356). New York, NY: Praeger.

Benn, S. I. (1983). Private and public morality clean living and dirty hands. In S. I. Benn & G. F. Gaus (Eds.), *Public and private in social life* (pp. 158–159). Harmondsworth: Penguin.

Berge, P. L., & Luckmann, T. (1967). *The social construction of reality*. New York, NY: Anchor.

Bettis, J. D. (1969). *Phenomenology of religion*. London: Student Christian Movement Press.

Bhaktivedanta Swami Prabhupāda, A. C. (1977). *Bhagavad-gita as it is*. Watford, ND: Bhaktivedanta Book Trust.

Billig, M. (1991). *Ideology and opinions: Studies in rhetorical psychology*. London: Sage Publications.

Billig, M., Condor, S., Edwards, D., Gane, M., Middleton, D., & Radley, A. (1988). *Ideological dilemmas: A social psychology of everyday thinking*. Thousand Oaks, CA: Sage Publications.

Bilsker, D., & Marcia, J. E. (1991). Adaptive regression and ego identity. *Journal of Adolescence, 14*(1), 75–84.

Bloom, B. S., & Committee of College and University Examiners. (1964). *Taxonomy of educational objectives* (Vol. 2). New York, NY: Longmans, Green.

Bonhoeffer, D. (1955). *Ethics*. London: Student Christian Movement.

Bradley, F. H. (1927). *Ethical studies*. Oxford: Oxford University Press.

Brandt, R. B. (1972). Utilitarianism and the rules of war. *Philosophy & Public Affairs, 1*(2), 145–165.

Brehm, J. W., & Cohen, A. R. (1962). *Explorations in cognitive dissonance*. London: John Wiley & Sons.

Brennan, J. (1977). *The open texture of moral concepts*. New York, NY: Macmillan.

Bruner, J. S. (1960). *The process of education*. Cambridge, MA: Harvard University Press.

Bruner, J. S. (1964). The course of cognitive growth. *American Psychologist, 19*(1), 1.

Camus, A. (1984). *The just: Caligula and other plays* (H. Jones, Trans.). Harmondsworth: Penguin.

Child, D. (1986). *Psychology and the teacher*. London: Cassell.

Clark, C., & Caffarella, R. (Eds.). (2000). *An update on adult development theory: New ways of thinking about the life course (New directions for adult and continuing education)*. San Francisco, CA: Jossey-Bass.

Cohen, L., & Manion, L. (1980). *Research methods in education*. London: Croom Helm.

Cohen, M. Z. (1987). A historical overview of the phenomenologic movement. *Journal of Nursing Scholarship, 19*(1), 31–34.

Commons, M. L., Richards, F. A., & Armon, C. (1984). *Beyond formal operations: Late adolescent and adult cognitive development*. New York, NY: Praeger.

REFERENCES

Conee, E. (1982). Against moral dilemmas. *The philosophical Review, 91*(1), 87–97.

Cronbach, L. J. (1957). The two disciplines of scientific psychology. *American Psychologist, 12*(11), 671.

Crook, J. (1985). A validation study of a self-directed learning readiness scale. *Journal of Nursing Education, 24*(7), 274–279.

Dalton, P., & Dunnett, G. (1992). *A psychology for living: Personal construct theory for professionals and clients.* Oxford: John Wiley.

Davidson, D. (2001). *Essays on actions and events: Philosophical essays* (Vol. 1). Oxford: Oxford University Press

Davis, G. A., & Rimm, S. B. (1988). *Education of the gifted and talented.* Englewood Cliffs, NJ: Prentice-Hall, Inc.

De Bono, E. (1977). *Lateral thinking: A textbook of creativity.* Harmondsworth: Penguin.

De Bono, E. (1981). *The mechanism of mind.* Harmondsworth: Penguin.

De Bono, E. (1982). *De Bono's thinking course.* London: BBC.

De Bono, E. (1987). *Six thinking hats.* Harmondsworth: Penguin.

Denzin, N. K. (1970). *The research act in sociology: A theoretical introduction to sociological method.* London: Butterworth.

Devlin, P. (1965). *The enforcement of morals.* Oxford: Oxford University Press.

Dewey, J. (1998). *How we think: A restatement of the relation of reflective thinking to the educative process.* Boston, MA: Houghton Mifflin.

Donagan, A. (1984). Consistency in rationalist moral systems. *The Journal of Philosophy, 81*(6), 291–309.

Duncker, K., & Lees, L. S. (1945). On problem-solving. *Psychological Monographs, 58*(5), 1–113.

Durkheim, E. (1962). *Moral education.* London: Routledge and Kegan Paul.

Edwards, D., & Potter, J. (1992). *Discursive psychology* (Vol. 8). London: Sage.

Engels, F. (1957). *Anti-dühring.* London: Lawrence and Wishart.

Erikson, E. H. (1959). *Childhood and society.* New York, NY: Norton.

Eysenck, H. J. (1985). The nature and measurement of intelligence. In J. Freeman (Ed.), *Psychology of gifted children.* New York, NY: John Wiley & Sons.

Festinger, L. (1957). *A theory of cognitive dissonance.* Standford, CA: Standford University Press.

Festinger, L. (1964). *Conflict, decision and dissonance.* London: Tavistock Publications.

Fletcher, J. (1966). *Situation ethics.* London: Student Christian Movement Press.

Flew, A. (1975). *Thinking about thinking.* London: Fontana.

Foot, P. (1983). Moral realism and moral dilemma. *The Journal of Philosophy, 80*(7), 379–398.

Fransson, G., & Grannäs, J. (2013). Dilemmatic spaces in educational contexts – towards a conceptual framework for dilemmas in teachers work. *Teachers and Teaching: Theory and Practice, 19*, 4–17.

Freud, S. (1901). Psychopathology of everyday life. In J. Strachey (Ed.), *The standard edition of the collected works* (Vol. 24). London: Hogarth Press.

Gaut, B. (1993). Moral pluralism. *Philosophical Papers, 22*(1), 17–40.

Gauthier, D. P. (1963). *Practical reasoning.* London: Oxford University Press.

George, W., Cohn, S., & Stanley, J. (1979). *Educating the gifted: Acceleration and enrichment: Revised and expanded proceedings of the ninth annual Hyman Blumberg symposium on research in early childhood education.* Baltimore, MD: Johns Hopkins University Press.

Getzels, J. W., & Jackson, P. W. (1962). *Creativity and intelligence: Explorations with gifted students.* New York, NY: John Wiley & Sons.

Gilhooly, K. J. (1982). *Thinking: Directed, undirected and creative.* London: Academic Press.

Gillon, R. (1994). Medical ethics: Four principles plus attention to scope. *British Medical Journal, 309*(6948), 184–188.

Glaser, B. G. (1967). *The discovery of grounded theory: Strategies for qualitative research.* New York, NY: Aldine.

Gowans, C. W. (Ed.). (1987). *Moral dilemmas.* New York, NY: Oxford University Press.

Guilford, J. P. (1950). Creativity. *American Psychologist, 5*, 444–454.

Guilford, J. P. (1956). The structure of the intellect. *Psychological Bulletin, 53*, 267–293.

Grant, G. E. (1988). *Teaching critical thinking.* New York, NY: Praeger.

Great Britain Department of Education and Science. (1977). Curriculum 11–16 [S.1.]: DES.

Greenspan, P. S. (1983). Moral dilemmas and guilt. *Philosophical Studies, 43*(1), 117–125.

Hamilton, D. L. E. (1981). *Cognitive processes in stereotyping and intergroup behaviour.* Hillsdale, NJ: Lawrence Erlbaum Associates.

Hampshire, S. (1978). *Public and private morality.* Cambridge: Cambridge University Press.

Hampshire, S. (1983). *Morality and conflict.* Oxford: Blackwell.

Hare, R. M. (1981). *Moral thinking.* Oxford: Oxford University Press.

Hegel, G. W. F. (1975a). *Logic.* Oxford: Clarendon.

Hegel, G. W. F. (1975b). *Aesthetics* (Vol. 2, T. M. Knox, Trans.). Oxford: Clarendon.

Hegel, G. W. F. (1977). *Phenomenology of spirit* (A. V. Miller, Trans.). Oxford: Clarendon.

Hirst, P. H. (1973). Liberal education and the nature of knowledge. In R. S. Peters (Ed.), *The philosophy of education.* Oxford: Oxford University Press.

Honig, B. (1996). Difference, dilemmas, and the politics of home. In S. Benhabib (Ed.), *Democracy and difference: Contesting the boundaries of the political* (pp. 257–277). Princeton, NJ: Princeton University Press.

Howatch, S. (1988). *Glittering images.* London: Fontana.

Ibesen, H. (1958). *A doll's house* (R. F. Sharp & E. M. Aveling, Trans.). London: J.M. Dent & Sons.

Illich, I. D. (1973). *Deschooling society.* Harmondsworth: Penguin.

Inhelder, B., & Piaget, J. (1958). *The growth of logical thinking from childhood to adolescent.* London: Routledge & Kegan Paul.

Janis, I., & Mann, L. (1977). *Decision making.* New York, NY: Free Press.

Jeffreys, M. V. C. (1950). *Glaucon: An inquiry into the aims of education.* London: Pitman.

Kant, I. (1929). *Fundamental principles of the metaphysic of ethics* (T. K. Abbott, Trans.). London: Longmans Green.

Kant, I. (1960). *Religion within the limits of reason alone* (T. Greene & H. Hudson, Trans.). New York, NY: Harper & Row.

Kant, I. (1969). *Groundwork of the metaphysics of morals* (J. Immelmann, Trans.). London: Hutchinson University Library.

Kant, I. (1971). *The doctrine of virtue: Part II of the metaphysic of morals* (M. J. Gregor, Trans.). Philadelphia, PA: University of Pennsylvania Press.

Kelly, G. (1970). A brief introduction to personal construct theory. In D. L. Bannister (Ed.), *Perspectives in personal construct theory.* London: Academic Press.

Kitchener, K. S., & King, P. M. (1981). Reflective judgment: Concepts of justification and their relationship to age and education. *Journal of Applied Developmental Psychology, 2*(2), 89–116.

Knaack, P. (1984). Phenomenological research. *Western Journal of Nursing Research, 6*(1), 107–114.

Kohlberg, L. (1966). Cognitive stages and preschool education. *Human Development, 9*(1–2), 5–17.

Kohlberg, L. (1981). *The philosophy of moral development.* New York, NY: Harper & Row.

Kohlberg, L. (1984). *The psychology of moral development.* New York, NY: Harper & Row.

Koplowitz, H. (1984). A projection beyond Piaget's formal operations stage: A general system stage and a unitary stage. In M. L. Commons, F. A. Richards, & C. Armon (Eds.), *Beyond formal operations: Late adolescent and adult cognitive development.* New York, NY: Praeger.

Kramer, D. A. (1983). Post-formal operations? A need for further conceptualization. *Human Development, 26*(2), 91–105.

Kurtines, W., & Greif, E. B. (1974). The development of moral thought: Review and evaluation of Kohlberg's approach. *Psychological Bulletin, 81*(8), 453.

Lactantius, L. C. F. (1871). *The divine institutes: The works of Lactantius* (Vol. 1, W. Fletcher, Trans.). Edinburg: T&T Clark.

Laertius, D. (1959). *Lives of eminent philosophers.* (R. D. Hicks, Trans.). London: Heinemann.

Lago, C., & Shipton, G. (1994). *On listening and learning.* London: Central Book Publishing.

Lemmon, E. J. (1962). Moral dilemmas. *The Philosophical Review, 70,* 139–158.

Lindsay, D. (1993). *The beggar's opera and other eighteenth-century plays.* London: Everyman.

Lorenz, K. (1966). *On aggression.* London: Methuen.

REFERENCES

Loughran, J. (2006). *Developing a pedagogy of teacher education: Understanding teaching and learning about teaching.* London: Routledge.

Loughran, J. (1999). *Researching teaching: Methodologies and practices for understanding pedagogy.* London: Falmer Press.

Louizos, V. (1994). *Emergent independence: The psychological status of older adolescents: Concerns, coping strategies and the changing role of parents* (Master thesis). University of Surrey, Guildford.

Lucas, J. R. (1966). *Principles of politics.* Oxford: Clarendon.

Machiavelli, N. (1965). *The Prince Machiavelli: The chief works and others* (Vol. 3, A. Gilbert, Trans.). Durham, NC: Duke University Press.

Macintyre, A. (1985). *After virtue: A study in moral theory.* London: Duckworth.

Mannheim, K. (1991). *Ideology and Utopia.* New York, NY: Routledge & Kegan Paul.

Marcia, J. E. (1980). Identity in adolescence. In J. Adelson (Ed.), *Handbook of adolescent psychology.* New York, NY: John Wiley & Sons.

Marcus, R. B. (1980). Moral dilemmas and consistency. *The Journal of Philosophy, 77*(3), 121–136.

Marland, S. P. (1972). *Education of the gifted and talented: Report to the congress of the United States by the U.S.* Wshington, DC: U.S. GPO.

Mayer, E. R. (1977). *Thinking and problem solving: An introduction to human cognition and learning.* Glenview, IL: Scott Foresman.

Mill, J. S. (1910). *Utilitarianism, liberty and representative government.* London: J.M. Dent & Sons.

Mill, J. S. (1974). *A system of logic ratiocinative and inductive.* Toronto: University of Toronto Press.

Nagel, T. (1972). War and massacre. *Philosophy & Public Affairs, 1*(2), 123–144.

Niebuhr, R. (1963). *Moral and immoral society.* London: Student Christian Movement Press.

Noonan, E. (1983). *Counselling young people.* London: Methuen.

Nussbaum, M. (1985). Aeschylus and practical conflict. *Ethics, 95,* 233–267.

Nussbaum, M. (1986). *The fragility of goodness.* Oxford: Oxford University Press.

Oakeshott, M. (1981). *Rationalism in politics.* New York, NY: Routledge and Chapman & Hall.

O'Hear, A. (1981). *Education, society and human nature.* London: Routledge.

Parfit, D. (1984). *Reasons and persons.* Oxford: Oxford University Press.

Parlett, M., & Dearden, G. (Eds.). (1981). *Introduction to illuminative evaluation: Studies in higher education.* Guildford: Society for Research into Higher Education.

Parlett, M., & Hamilton, D. (1981). Evaluation as illumination. In M. Parlett & G. Dearden (Eds.), *Introduction to illuminative evaluation: Studies in higher education.* Guildford: Society for Research into Higher.

Parnes, S. J., Noller, R. B., & Biondi, A. M. (1977). *Guide to creative action.* New York, NY: Scribner.

Parsons, T. (1991). *The social system.* London: Routledge & Kegan Paul.

Pascal, B. (1955). *Pensees.* London: Nelson.

Paterson, J., & Zderad, L. (1976). *Humanistic nursing.* New York, NY: John Wiley & Sons.

Perry, W. G. (1968). *Forms of intellectual and ethical development in the college years.* New York, NY: Holt, Rinehart and Winston.

Peters, R. S. (1964). *Education as initiation.* London: Evans Bros.

Peters, R. S. (1965). Education as initiation. In R. D. Archambault (Ed.), *Philosophical analysis and education.* New York, NY: Humanities Press.

Peters, R. S. (1966). *Ethics and education.* London: Allen & Unwin.

Peters, R. S. (1973). *The philosophy of education.* Oxford: Oxford University Press.

Peters, R. S. (1981). *Moral development and moral education.* London: Allen & Unwin.

Phenix, P. H. (1964). *Realms of meaning: A philosophy of the curriculum for general education.* New York, NY: McGraw Hill.

Piaget, J. (1932). *The moral judgment of the child.* London: Routledge & Kegan Paul.

Plato. (1974). *The republic* (D. Lee, Trans.). Harmondsworth: Penguin.

Postman, N., & Weingartner, C. (1971). *Teaching as a subversive activity.* Harmondsworth: Penguin.

Potter, J., & Wetherell, M. (1987). *Discourse and social psychology.* London: Sage.

Quintilian. (1958). *The institutio oratorio of quintilia.* London: Heinemann.

Raphael, D. D. (1975). The standards of morals. *Proceedings of the Aristotelian Society, 75,* 1–12.

Rawls, J. (1971). *A theory of justice.* Cambridge, MA: Harvard University Press.

Renzulli, J. S. (1977). *The enrichment triad model: A guide for developing defensible programs for the gifted and talented.* Wethersfield, CT: Creative Learning Press.

Rhymes, D. (1964). *No new morality: Christian personal values and sexual morality.* London: Constable.

Ross, W. D. (1930). *The right and the good.* Oxford: Oxford University Press.

Rossiter, M. (1999). Understanding adult development as narrative. In M. C. Clark & R. S. Caffarella (Eds.), *An update on adult development theory: New ways of thinking about the life course (New directions for adult and continuing education).* San Francisco, CA: Jossey-Bass.

Russell, T., & Bullock, S. (1999). Discovering our professional knowledge as teachers: Critical dialogues about learning from experience. In J. Loughran (Ed.), *Researching teaching: Methodologies and practices for understanding pedagogy.* London: Falmer Press.

Rybash, J. M., Hoyer, W. J., & Roodin, P. A. (1986). *Adult cognition and aging: Developmental changes in processing, knowing and thinking.* Oxford: Pergamon Press.

Ryle, G. (1954). *Dilemmas.* Cambridge: Cambridge University Press.

Sartre, J. P. (1948). *L'existentialisme est une humanisme* (P. Mairet, Trans.). London: Methuen.

Sartre, J. P. (1955). *Dirty hands: No exit and three other plays* (L. Abel, Trans.). New York, NY: Vintage Books.

Schonsheck, J. (1991). Nuclear stalemate: A superior escape from the dilemmas of deterrence. *Philosophy and Public Affairs, 20,* 35–51.

Searle, J. (1978). Prima facie obligations. In J. Raz (Ed.), *Practical reasoning* (p. 81). Oxford: Oxford University Press.

Shaw, B. (1994). *Major Barbara.* Harmondsworth: Penguin.

Shope, R. K. (1965). Prima facie duty. *The Journal of Philosophy, 62*(11), 279–287.

Sinnott-Armstrong, W. (1985). Moral dilemmas and incomparability. *American Philosophical Quarterly, 22*(4), 321–329.

Sinnott, J. D. (1984). Postformal reasoning: The relative stage. In M. L. Commons, F. A. Richards, & C. Armon (Eds.), *Beyond formal operations: Late adolescent and adult cognitive development.* New York, NY: Praeger.

Slote, M. (1985). Utilitarianism, moral dilemmas, and moral cost. *American Philosophical Quarterly, 22*(2), 161–168.

Sophocles. (1962). *Three tragedies: Antigone, Oedipus the king, Electra* (H. D. F. Kitto, Trans.). Oxford: Oxford University Press.

Spearman, C. (1904). General intelligence, objectively determined and measured. *The American Journal of Psychology, 15*(2), 201–292.

Spedding, J., Ellis, R. L., & Heath, D. D. (1901). *The works of Francis Bacon.* London: Longmans.

Statman, D. (1990). The debate over the so-called reality of moral dilemmas. *Philosophical Papers, 19*(3), 191–211.

Stebbing, S. (1965). *A modern elementary logic.* London: Methuen.

Sternberg, R. J. (1985). *Beyond I.Q.* Cambridge: Cambridge University Press.

Sternberg, R. J. (1986). *Critical thinking: Its nature, measurement and improvement.* Washington, DC: National Institute of Education.

Sternberg, R. J., & Davidson, J. (1986). *Conceptions of giftedness.* New York, NY: Cambridge University Press.

Styron, W. (1980). *Sophie's choice.* New York, NY: Bantam.

Tallentyre, S. G. (1907). *The friends of Voltaire.* New York, NY: G.P. Putnams's Sons.

Taylor, K. (1999). Development as separation and connection: Finding a balance. In M. C. Clark & R. S. Caffarella (Eds.), *An update on adult development theory: New ways of thinking about the life course (New directions for adult and continuing education).* San Francisco, CA: Jossey-Bass.

Tertullianus, Q. S. F. (1969). *The writings of quintus sept. Flor.* Edinburgh: T&T Clark.

Tertullian, Q. S. F. (1931). *Apology* (T. R. Glover, Trans.). London: Heinemann.

Trigg, R. (1971). Moral conflict. *Mind, 80*(317), 41–55.

United Kingdom. (1957). *Report of the committee on homosexual offences and prostitution* (p. 95). London: Her Majesty's Stationery Office.

REFERENCES

Van Gelder, T. J. (1989). Credible threats and usable weapons: Some dilemmas of deterrence. *Philosophy & Public Affairs, 18*(2), 158–183.

Vernon, P. E. (1942). *Groundwork of educational theory*. London: Chambers Harrap Publishers Ltd.

Wallach, M. A., & Kogan, N. (1965). *Modes of thinking in young children*. New York, NY: Holt, Rinehart and Wilson.

Walzer, M. (1973). Political action: The problem of dirty hands. *Philosophy & Public Affairs, 2*(2), 160–180.

Warnock, G. J. (1967). *Contemporary moral philosophy*. London: Macmillan.

Weber, H. (1970). *Essays in sociology* (H. H. Gerth & C. W. Mills, Trans.). London: Routledge & Kegan Paul.

Weber, M. (1948). Politics as a vocation. In H. H. Gerth & C. W. Mills (Eds.), *From Max Weber: Essays in sociology*. London: Kegan Paul, Trench, and Trubner.

Williams, B. (1973). *Problems of the self: Philosophical papers 1956–1972*. Cambridge: Cambridge University Press.

Winnicott, D. W. (1968). *The family and individual development*. London: Tavistock Publications.

Winter, R. (1982). Dilemma analysis: A contribution to methodology for action research. *Cambridge Journal of Education, 12*(3), 161–174.

Winter, R. (1989). *Learning from experience*. Lewes: Falmer Press.

Wood, P., Hymer, B., & Michel, D. (2007). *Dilemma-based learning in the humanities: Integrating social, emotional and thinking skills*. London: Chris Kington Publishing.

INDEX